STUDENT TESTIMONIALS

Having the pleasure of learning under Mr. Garcia's leadership, was truly a highlight of my education. I am in awe of his experiences and expertise in many of his endeavors. Mr. Garcia has a true passion for leadership. He shares his vision of leadership in a way that sticks with his students. My favorite visual is the *Leadership Pyramid*, which depicts of how supporting the mission, caring for the people and putting your own ego aside, makes for high achievement and respect in a company. Another thing he mentioned is "You cannot lead unless you know how to follow." What a powerful statement! He taught us natural leaders lead no matter what title they hold. His open-door policy and personable manner make it very easy to see that he practices what he teaches. It is safe to speak on behalf of my classmates as well that, Mr. Garcia is well respected and his teachings are something to treasure. A "thank you" is not enough for Mr. Garcia's service to our country and his willingness to teach future leaders.

— Wendy Razzano, Empire State College 2019

As a recent graduate of college and fresh into the work force I am grateful for the lessons learned from Mr. Garcia. I often reflected on principles learned in class to be the best employee and leader I can. Unlike other teachers of leadership Mr. Garcia does a great job of using his real-life experience in both the military and business sectors to prepare students for what they will face as new hires in business.

— Kyle Weaver, Citadel Class of 2016

Professor Garcia's Leadership in Organizations class taught me important lessons that still resonate today, even several years removed from graduation. His prior experience in both military and financial sectors provided many examples of leadership and followership opportunities that I could, and did, face in the business world. In the transitions from The Citadel to graduate school to a Big 4 accounting firm, Professor Garcia's concepts provided me with a strong academic foundation to continually draw from throughout my professional development.

— Paul Barringer, Citadel Class of 2015

Dedication

To all the students in my leadership classes, whose positive feedback to the lessons taught became the inspiration to write this book, and to every new college graduate entering the workforce – that they make a positive difference every day.

Table of Contents

Foreword i
Introduction iii
Chapter 1: Meet your boss halfway (but *you will* work harder) 1
Chapter 2: Develop your "leadership signature" 11
Chapter 3: A good leader should LISTEN 47
Chapter 4: Climb the Leader's Pyramid (for balance and
 consistency) 57
Chapter 5: Manage your ego (as one manages cholesterol) 75
Chapter 6: Diversity: A complete leader leads all people 81
Chapter 7: Using creativity to solve problems 89
Chapter 8: Knowledge is on a learning curve, character on
 a straight line 109
Chapter 9: Lane Management 115
Chapter 10: Using the APE theory 123
Conclusion 137
Acknowledgements 139

Foreword

PRIOR TO BECOMING the ninth President at Elon, I proudly served as the Provost and Dean of the College at The Citadel in Charleston, South Carolina. While there, I first met and had the privilege to serve alongside Joe Garcia, the Vice President for Finance and Business. I was drawn to the Citadel because of its strong student success and leadership development model which had led to so many successful graduates over the years. In fact, the *U.S. News and World Report's* Best College Rankings identified The Citadel as the #1 southern regional masters public college because of its strong reputation and success in outpacing students' predicted graduation rates.

Joe's book, his fourth, *When the Cap Falls: Ten principles for a college graduate to launch a career* is an essential read for new college graduates entering today's workforce. Each year, approximately three million college students will graduate with some type of degree, from an associates to a doctoral degree. Yet, many hiring managers cite a lack of "soft skills" such as critical thinking, problem solving, leadership, coaching, and teamwork for recent college graduates. *When the Cap Falls* attempts to close that gap by providing engaging, original, and interactive concepts for the new college graduate.

While other authors target college graduates, their advice often centers around general post-graduation advice like resume writing, interview skills, salary negotiation, etc. Joe's book is unique because it directly addresses the *soft skills* gap that hiring managers say exist with new college graduates. His guidance leverages Joe's uncommon breadth of experience that includes: a distinguished military career, senior positions in the federal government, private sector consulting, non-profit board chair duties, and higher education cabinet-level positions. His many awards include Male Boss of the Year from the Federal Woman's Program.

Joe taught leadership courses as an adjunct instructor at the Air Force Academy and The Citadel, where the ten principles highlighted in this book received favorable student feedback. I had the firsthand opportunity to see him teach in the classroom. Ever the innovator, Joe established small group problem solving teams where cadets would take on leadership challenges being experienced across campus. Through his guidance and encouragement, the cadets made thoughtful recommendations on how to improve their learning and living environment at The Citadel. Many of their recommendations led to real change and improvement, both academically and in the other core pillars such as military training. Joe's end-of-course student surveys were always outstanding. His passion and commitment to our students, both in the classroom and as a mentor, always stood out to me.

His commitment to student success is why I wholeheartedly endorse Joe's latest book, *When the Cap Falls: Ten principles for a college graduate to launch a career*. His insight is shared, as he did in the classroom, in an easy-to-follow but impactful way that will give new college graduates an important advantage in the workplace. Any leader, whether novice, seasoned or mid-career, would benefit from Joe's many years of successful leadership. I know I did.

Constance L. Book

Connie Book
President, Elon University

Introduction

> "I think a college education is important no matter what you do in life."
>
> *Phil Mickelson, professional golfer*

THERE IS NO doubt about it. A college education dramatically changed my life for the better. My parents, both hard-working people, did not even attend high school and often struggled economically. I was more fortunate, as doors opened for me when I earned my Bachelor's degree, followed by two Master's degrees. Each time, there was a direct benefit from the knowledge acquired through a college education.

As you obtain your own degree, whether Associates, Bachelor's, Master's, or even PhD, today's employers are looking for well-rounded individuals who possess both technical expertise and the "soft skills" to be successful in the workplace. In a *Washington Post* article, "The surprising thing Google learned about its employees — and what it means for today's students," Valerie Strauss elaborated on this notion.[1]

In a research project called Project Oxygen, technology giant Google looked back since its founding in 1998 to determine the best qualities associated with its top employees. Surprisingly, for a

---

1 *The Washington Post*, December 20, 2017

company now associated with self-driving cars, STEM came in last on the list of the top eight qualities. Instead, the study showed that the following attributes were even more important:[2]

- Being a good coach
- Communication skills
- Possessing insights into others and different values and points of view
- Empathy
- Critical thinking
- Problem solving
- Drawing conclusions (making connections across complex ideas)

In another study, this time a Workforce-Skills Preparedness Report, hiring managers identified the most commonly lacking soft skills in recent college graduates. Like the Google's study of their own employees, the second list includes the following:[3]

- Critical thinking/problem solving
- Attention to detail
- Communication
- Ownership
- Leadership
- Interpersonal skills/teamwork
- Grit
- Curiosity

With the two lists in mind, my purpose in writing this book is to share easy-to-remember, and therefore easy-to-apply principles as you earn your college degree and advance in the workplace. These

---

2   Ibid.
3   "Leveling Up: How to Win In the Skills Economy," the 2016 Workforce-Skills Preparedness Report

principles helped me succeed in an uncommon breadth of challenging assignments, including a military career, senior employment for the federal government, private sector consulting, board chairman for several nonprofits, and Cabinet-level positions in higher education.

My time in higher education is especially significant. Even though I served in administration leadership positions at several colleges, my time as a leadership instructor at the United States Air Force Academy, The Citadel, The Military College of South Carolina, and SUNY Empire State College became the incubator for the ten principles in this book.

Leveraging my experiences that ranged from being the "Katrina CFO" in New Orleans for three years after that devastating storm to a military deployment in the Middle East, I developed valuable lessons for students who were preparing to graduate. Their positive feedback inspired me to write this book.

Most of the principles you will read are original in nature, not to be found in other leadership books. Some of the chapters are brief, only a few pages long, while others longer. Here is a summary and synopsis of the ten principles that we will be reviewing:

First Principle: Meet your boss halfway (but *you'll* work harder)

As you start a career, you will need to work effectively with your boss. We discuss that when meeting your boss in the middle, you will still have to work harder to get there. I will explain why this is the case and offer tips on being a good follower.

Second Principle: Develop your "leadership signature"

Using a fun and interactive approach in this chapter, we discuss the five available powers a leader possesses and how to use them. The five fingers of your hand are analogous to the different powers. The concept was originally presented in my book, *Talk to the Hand: Being a great leader is at your fingertips*.

Third Principle: A good leader should LISTEN

In this chapter, we review why it is so important to listen to others, barriers that exist, and ways to improve your listening skills. The LISTEN acronym is a helpful way to apply this important principle.

Fourth Principle: Climb the Leader's Pyramid (for balance and consistency)

This original concept put forth in my book *The Leader's Pyramid: a balanced and consistent approach to leadership*, is especially valuable to a new graduate and future leader. The Leader's Pyramid principle provides consistency and balance across the mission, people concerns, and our ego.

Fifth Principle: Manage your ego (as one manages cholesterol)

Every one of us has good and bad ego, in the same manner we all have good and bad cholesterol flowing through our veins. Similarly, we acknowledge that good ego can produce necessary self-confidence, whereas bad ego (like bad cholesterol) can lead to negative effects.

Sixth Principle: Diversity: A complete leader leads all people

No person can do it alone. We need the capacity of the entire team to achieve organizational goals. A complete leader ensures everyone participates, so that everyone can contribute.

Seventh Principle: Using creativity to solve problems

One of my favorite principles, this chapter addresses the number one soft skill that hiring managers feel college graduates are lacking per the Workforce-Skills Preparedness Report. We discuss how a leader should approach problems with a positive mindset to seek multiple options. Leveraging group diversity can also help generate innovative ideas to solve problems.

Eighth Principle: Knowledge is on a learning curve, character on a straight line

As you begin your career, you will ride a natural learning curve when it comes to gaining knowledge of your profession. However, this chapter stresses the necessity that your character should not be on a learning curve, but on a straight line. Your integrity should always be high and remain so throughout your career.

Ninth Principle: Lane Management

Avid swimmers learn the basics of swim lane etiquette when there is not a single lane per swimmer at practice or when at a community pool. In this chapter, we discuss the principle of lane management at work, especially with your peer group. Being a good teammate is critical to organizational success that benefits everyone.

Tenth Principle: Use the APE theory

My third book, *Leading in the Jungle: a fable of a chimp's quest to lead like a gorilla*, introduced a concept that I call the APE theory. This last principle is one that effectively captures many of the earlier concepts, including individual Accountability, Partnering with others, and that Everyone is important.

The goal is that these ten principles will give you a head start, a foundation to build upon, as you develop a leadership style based on your own experience. As Leonardo da Vinci once said, "Wisdom is the daughter of experience." Put another way, from experience comes wisdom. In the meantime, I am eager to share mine with you.

Let's get started.

CHAPTER 1

Meet your boss halfway (but *you will* work harder)

"The first thing the secretary types is the boss."

Donald Trump

ONE OF THE biggest challenges I had in my own career was being able to work effectively with my various bosses. When I started as an enlisted person in the Air Force, I was a decent follower. However, when I became an officer and a leader in my own right, I continually struggled with too many bosses. I had a simple but very misguided belief.

My boss should always be a better leader than I am as a leader.

The problem with that perspective is that my view factors in only what goes on in my limited world – not that of the supervisor. Big mistake.

Therefore, the first principle for a new college graduate that we start with is not a motivation or coaching technique that one would normally think of for a leadership book. We begin instead with the importance of being a good follower.

Similarly, one of the first lessons of the semester in my leadership class I taught at The Citadel was "working with the boss." I let my class know that I was not proud of my record of accomplishment as a follower. In fact, my immature actions were an embarrassment. My objective was for my class to avoid the type of mistakes that I had made. This type of advice was the benefit that I brought into the classroom as an adjunct instructor – real world experience.

Getting in front of the students was a challenge. Remember, I was the Vice President for Finance and Business and Chief Financial Officer at The Citadel, a full-time member of the President's Cabinet, and a challenging position. I had petitioned the President (a retired three-star general) to teach leadership courses as I had done previously at the Air Force Academy. He needed a Chief Financial Officer (my key role), and not another instructor which he had plenty. In the end, I balanced my primary role and the adjunct instructor role without a problem.

Interacting with the students (cadets in this case), also allowed me to better understand our primary mission at the military college. By teaching the course, I gained valuable insight to what was occurring throughout the South Carolina Corps of Cadets. It also gave me a chance to develop a mentor relationship with many students that often went beyond their graduation date.

My end-of-course student surveys were among the highest in the School of Business, and the "boss-follower lesson" routinely received particularly high marks.

Every semester, I arranged for a special guest speaker, Sergeant Major Andrew Yaegle, United States Marine Corps (retired), to supplement the lesson. The Sergeant Major was a key leader in his own right at The Citadel, assisting the Commandant of Cadets in the development of principled leaders. He had a stellar active duty military career, including numerous overseas deployments. His many awards and decorations including: Legion of Merit Medal, Meritorious Service Medal with one gold star, Navy Marine Corps Commendation Medal with one gold star, the Navy Marine Corps Achievement Medal with three gold stars, and Combat "V" and Combat Action Ribbon.

While the entire Corps of Cadets respected his *leadership* ability, what made Sergeant Major Yaegle's talk to the cadets a more powerful lesson was his *followership* role supporting the Commandant of Cadets, normally a full Colonel position. The Sergeant Major shared not only how he strived to make that relationship work, but he went on to use other examples from his distinguished military career. As I sat in the audience with the cadets, I could see they held on to his every word. I took two primary takeaways from the Sergeant Major's sage wisdom.

- Have the moral courage to speak up and provide feedback to the boss
- Never cross the line by being disrespectful or insubordinate

The two lessons require a delicate balancing act. On one hand, every boss has a leadership blind spot, sometimes unaware the impact or consequence of a poor decision. You owe it to a boss to speak up when others may be reluctant to do so. I value a follower who looks at a potential decision and points out the risk. That is the moral courage part. In his book, *Outstanding!: 47 ways to make your organization exceptional*, bestselling author John G. Miller noted, "… ultimately, it's up to each of us as individuals to stand up and share what's on our mind. For that, let's look to ourselves and continually work to develop the courage necessary to do so. It's not always easy, but it's better for the organization – and for each of us."[4]

On the other hand, bosses can be sensitive to perceived criticism from a subordinate. Provide your feedback, but then as we used to say in the military "salute smartly" and move on. You may not always respect the person, but always respect the position.

As a new graduate, you may be eager to take on management

---

[4] John Miller, *Outstanding!: 47 ways to make your organization exceptional* (New York: Penguin Group, 2010), 37.

responsibilities, but you must learn to work *for* a boss first. Most new graduates will have had a boss of some kind in their life. This would be especially so of the non-traditional adult student who may be working full-time while going to school part-time (the kind that Empire State College educates). For the traditional student, who enters college right out of high school, there are probably part-time jobs or even volunteer work that meant dealing with a boss.

There are many reasons why a follower might not get along with a supervisor. The boss may be overly demanding in exercising his or her authority. Maybe the manager has little experience leading people and you are part of the learning curve. On the other hand, it takes two to tango and like on the dance floor you both cannot lead.

It is only natural for a follower to second-guess a supervisor's decision or even their management style. The problem exacerbates when a *group* of followers joins in the boss bashing – feeding off each other's remarks. Admittedly, I did my share of this type of sideline coaching.

Sideline is the key word. Imagine if work was like being suited up for a football contest and you refused to get in the game. Your boss, and some of your peers, are blocking, tackling, chasing a fumble and getting dirty or even bloodied. At the end of the game, you may have a nice clean jersey but that is only because you were not engaged on the field.

Read carefully the words of President Theodore Roosevelt around this concept:

> "It is not the critic who counts; not the man who points out how the strong man stumbles, or where the doer of deeds could have done them better. The credit belongs to the man who is actually in the arena, whose face is marred by dust and sweat and blood; who strives valiantly; who errs, who comes short again and again, because there is no effort without error and shortcoming; but who does actually strive to do

the deeds; who knows great enthusiasms, the great devotions; who spends himself in a worthy cause; who at the best knows in the end the triumph of high achievement, and who at the worst, if he fails, at least fails while daring greatly, so that his place shall never be with those cold and timid souls who neither know victory nor defeat."[5]

Recognize that your boss is constantly in the arena. The fallacy of the erroneous belief that my boss should always be a better leader was that I did not recognize the battles that he or she fights every day. For example, that last-minute task from my boss that I criticized may have likely come from *his or her* boss. In my military time, that could mean a general officer. The boss should not have to explain why he or she is asking you to do something.

Let us look at a sample organizational chart.

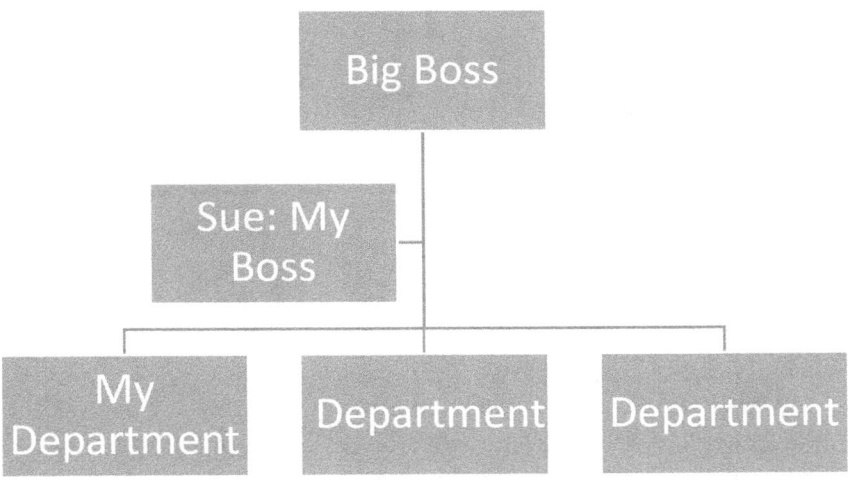

---

[5] Almanac of Theodore Roosevelt, website http://www.theodore-roosevelt.com/trsorbonnespeech.html

In this case, my imaginary boss Sue works for someone that I label simply as the "big boss." That person could oversee the entire company, a major division, etc. As shown, I have my own department, and work alongside two other departments that report to Sue.

Wrong Perspective

In my original thinking, I would expect Sue to meet me halfway in our relationship. Normally, that would look like the following:

It took a while, but here is what I finally realized. It was unfair for me to judge the actions or inactions of my boss compared to my own leadership responsibilities. In the sample organization chart, I only had to worry about one box - mine. My boss, Sue, on the other hand, had to worry about *all* the boxes on the organizational chart: Sue's, mine, the other departments, and the big boss. That is a 5 to 1 ratio!

Therefore, if we look at it from the organization chart perspective, meeting in the middle between Sue and me takes on a completely new meaning.

Right Perspective

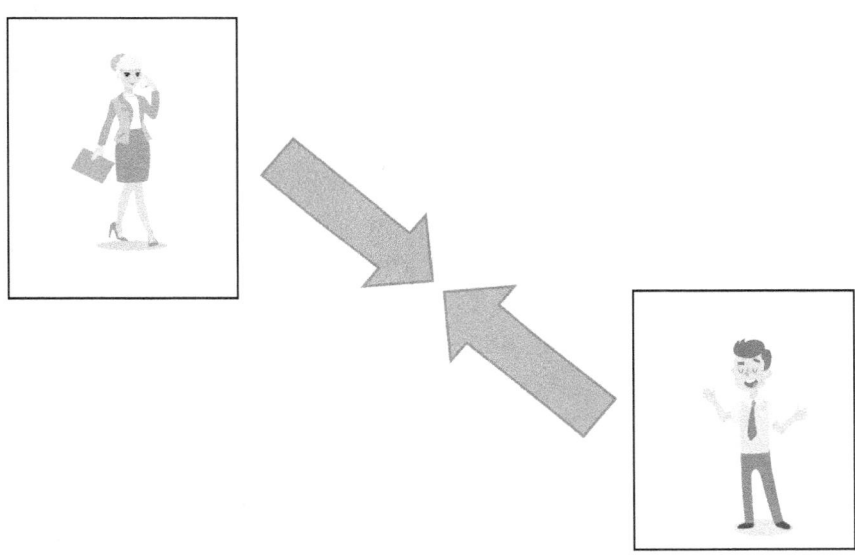

Notice, that in the second scenario, we are still meeting in the middle, but I now account for the differences in the organizational chart. Sue has more responsibilities and demands than I do. Therefore, even though we can still meet halfway, I need to work harder (pushing upward to get there).

I encourage all new college graduates to recognize that being a leader will have many challenges as well as rewards. When evaluating your boss (and we all will do), be mindful that he or she will inherently have additional demands than what you face.

In summary, my experience is that followers perform better when they engage proactively and positively with their boss. When necessary speak up, always be respectful, and meet your boss halfway – but the burden is ultimately on you to make the relationship work. Your career success will be very dependent on this first principle.

Tips for meeting your boss "halfway"

On an ongoing basis:
- Bring solutions, not just problems to your boss
- Follow-up periodically, drop by to report how things are going from your end
- A quick hello to see how the boss' day is going (even bosses need encouragement)
- Ask if you can assist in any way, you might get a special project opportunity

If your boss is already in place and you are the one reporting in for a new job:
- Get on the boss' calendar within the first week (30 minutes)
- Do your homework, find out as much as possible about the boss and the role he or she is currently in (areas supervised, etc.)
- Have a one-page resume that captures your education, work experience, interests, etc. (only hand over when your meeting is about to end)
- Ask your boss what types of challenges being faced and how you can help
- Find out how your boss likes to communicate (drop by in person, email, etc.)
- Tell your boss that you seek honest and candid feedback, you are open to suggestions to be a better performer
- Be prepared to respond in case you are asked what your career goals are
- Thank the boss for the opportunity to join the team

If you are in place, and the boss is new:
- Get on the boss' calendar within the first week (30 minutes)
- Do your homework, find out as much as possible about the boss's previous experience, education, etc.

- Try and develop initial rapport (ask how he/she likes the area, based on conversation, recommend a favorite restaurant or place of interest)
- Have a one-page resume that captures your education, work experience, interests, etc. (only hand over when your meeting is about to end)
- Be prepared to respond to what type of challenges or positive things are going on in your area
- Find out how your boss likes to communicate (email, phone call, etc.)
- Tell your boss that you seek honest and candid feedback, you are open to suggestions to be a better performer
- Be prepared to respond in case you are asked what your career goals are
- Welcome the boss to the organization and wish him/her success and you are there to provide any information or otherwise assist as needed
- Ask how the boss' transition is going, new housing, and schools for kids, etc.

CHAPTER **2**

Develop your "leadership signature"

"A basketball team is like the five fingers on your hand. If you can get them all together, you have a fist. That's how I want you to play."

Mike Krzyzewski, Hall of Fame Duke Basketball Coach

THE SECOND LEADERSHIP principle involves effectively using the power that is available to you. We begin this chapter with a signature test. Take a blank paper and draw two horizontal lines in the following manner:

―――――――――――――――――――

―――――――――――――――――――

Tightly clench your hand into a fist (whichever one you would normally use for a signature), with knuckles facing towards you. It would be as if you were going to "fist bump" somebody.

Next, still clenching a tight fist, fully extend only two fingers, the middle finger and the ring finger (next to your pinky). It should look like a pair of rabbit ears.

Now, take a pencil or pen, and place between your two extended fingers, keeping the other fingers clenched tightly.

Without the use of *any* other fingers, just the middle and ring fingers, write your signature on the top line of the two that you drew earlier.

Next, unclench your hand, and on the second line underneath, write your signature normally using all five fingers.

I asked my wife Brenda to take the test. For the first signature, she struggled to keep the pen stable and balanced. Thus, it is choppy and does not represent her true signature.

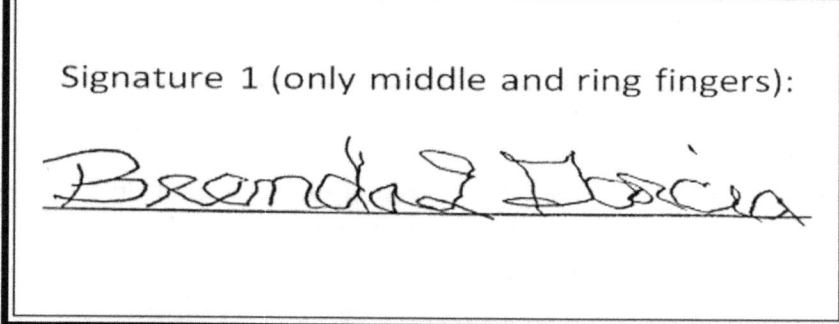

I then asked Brenda to write a second signature but this time using all her fingers. Without hesitation, she wrote her name naturally and with ease.

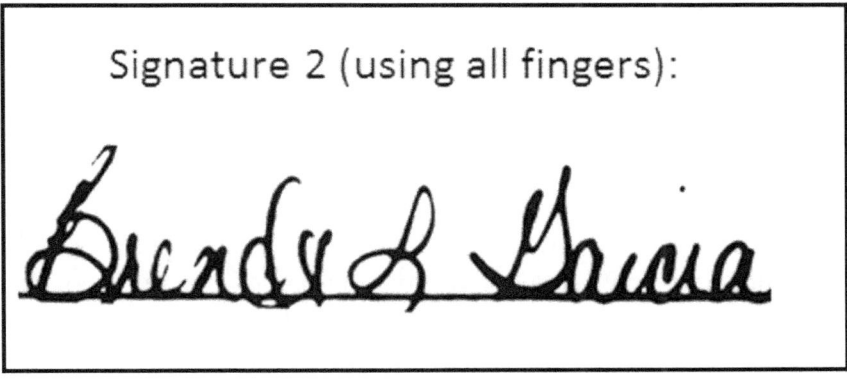

The difference between Brenda's first and second signature is striking. If you did the signature test properly, you too should see a difference when comparing your first signature with the second one.

Here is the implication of the signature test and the relation to leadership powers.

- The Signature Test shows that you limit the ability for your best signature by not using all available fingers.

- In the same manner, you limit your best leadership performance when you do not use all available influence powers.

While teaching a leadership course at the United States Air Force Academy, one of the lessons involved the use of power and influence. Per our textbook, there were five bases of power. Two social scientists named John R. P. French Jr. and Bertram Raven put forth the concept in an article entitled "The Bases of Social power" back in 1959.[6]

---

6   Richard Hughes, Robert Ginnett, and Gordon Curphy, *Leadership: Enhancing the Lessons of Experience* (New York: McGraw Hill, 2015), 123.

The five available forms of power identified by French and Raven are:

- Reward power
- Expert power
- Coercive power
- Legitimate power
- Referent power

As I prepared for the lesson, I tried to think of a way for the cadets to remember the five power bases as this was an important lesson in my mind. After some thought, an idea hit me. The five powers have a correlation to the five fingers on our hand. Modifying the terminology a bit but keeping the spirit of the meaning of each, I offered the following analogy to the various fingers.

- Reward power (thumb)
- Knowledge power (index finger)
- Discipline power (middle finger)
- Authority power (ring finger)
- Relationship power (pinky finger)

In the following examples, we use various fingers or a combination to act or make gestures that others can understand. You might be able to come up with your own list to supplement mine, but you will get the idea.

- To throw a Frisbee – use thumb, middle, and index fingers
- Make music on a piano or flute – every finger is used
- "Call me" gesture – thumb and pinky
- Vulcan salute – all fingers are used but the middle and ring fingers are parted
- Text a message – normally just thumbs
- Operating a TV remote – thumb and other fingers

DEVELOP YOUR "LEADERSHIP SIGNATURE"

- Shake hands – all fingers
- Putting a thread into a needle – thumb and index fingers
- Putting in your eye contacts – index and middle fingers

These few examples demonstrate a logical and natural balance among all or a combination of fingers we use. Using one finger (or several) does not limit your ability to use the others later. In the same manner, a leader should strive to use the full range of his or her powers per the situation at hand. Now that I described the general concept, we can be more specific for each of the powers demonstrated by our fingers.

Thumbs up: Using Rewards

> "Leaders who figure out, on their own, ways to reward their people for good performance get more good performance than leaders who run around all day putting out fires caused by their people's poor performance."[7]
>
> *Steve Chandler, from the book 100 Ways to Motivate Others*

An old Chinese custom used thumbs up to express respect. During World War II, American pilots would give a thumb up signal to communicate to their ground crews that everything was in order and they were ready to take off down the runway. Regardless of origin, in our case, the upright thumb gesture represents use of rewards for a job well done.

As part of a leader's ability to influence followers, the capacity to reward them is vital. Not using rewards would be like not using your thumb – reducing your ability to use your hand to the fullest capacity.

Your cell phone is likely close by so to illustrate, try texting a message without using your thumbs. Choose a family member or friend and send your text message using only the other four fingers besides your thumbs. You will likely get a puzzled response back because of the unusual auto-corrections necessary by not using your thumbs as you normally would.

Also, see how far you can throw a football without being able to use your thumb on your throwing hand. The thumb provides the necessary balance on one side of the football while you use the other four on the thread. Without the use of his thumb, quarterback Doug Flutie would not have been able to throw his famous "Hail Mary" pass nearly 70 yards as the game clock wound down to enable Boston College to beat the University of Miami Hurricanes on November 23, 1984.

Similarly, without the use of rewards, a leader is less capable of achieving maximum results. Rewards do not always have to be costly

---

[7] Steve Chandler, *100 ways to motivate others: How great leaders can produce insane results without driving people crazy* (Franklin Lakes: Career Press, 2008), 156

or time consuming to administer to make a difference. Sometimes an intangible reward can be as powerful as a tangible one. While a Captain in the Air Force, I received orders to Ramstein Air Base, Germany. The week I arrived to take charge of the largest Finance Office in Europe, was by coincidence the week that our unit was conducting their annual fitness test – a timed mile and a half run.

Despite being a bit older than most of the younger troops, I issued a challenge that if anyone could beat my time, I would offer a one-day pass. I was an avid runner at the time and figured that only a few could outdo me and that it would be a good morale booster for the unit.

At the midpoint of the run, only three runners out of many were ahead of me. The first two had a good lead and I would unlikely be able to catch up to them. However, I had my sights on the one Airman immediately in front of me, known as "Skip." Over 6 feet tall and weighing about 220 pounds, Skip looked more like a football lineman than the other two who were leading the pack. I thought for sure that he would slow down as the race wore on.

With only a few hundred yards to go, and the finish line in sight, I began to make my move. As I increased my pace, Skip kept looking over his shoulder and sped up so that I never did catch him. After the race, I walked over to shake his hand and congratulate him on his accomplishment. I confessed to him that I thought he would surely fade, and I would beat him. The young troop looked at me and said, "I kept thinking about that one day pass you had offered if we could beat you. I was tired, but I couldn't give up. I really wanted that one day pass."

Not everyone felt as Skip did about running hard just for a day pass. He gained more than just time off though, Skip gained bragging rights over me that he could playfully throw my way when the occasion warranted. To me, that was fine too, it would only motivate me the next time to do better.

As a new graduate, if you are able, look for ways to distribute rewards in your department. As my story with Skip demonstrates, a leader should be creative in the types of rewards that are used. For example, offering a hard-working employee to take off an hour early means more than you might imagine. Think of what someone can do with that hour.

- Get a manicure
- Beat traffic home
- Go grocery shopping
- Visit the library
- Workout at the gym
- Take a walk in the park
- Mow the lawn
- Get the car washed
- Grab a cup of coffee and read the newspaper
- Take a power nap
- Go to the driving range
- Catch up on homework if taking a night-time course

A recognition program is important. As John Kotter, respected management author and former Harvard Business School professor once noted, "…good leaders recognize and reward success, which not only gives people a sense of accomplishment but also makes them feel like they belong to an organization that cares about them."[8]

As the "Katrina CFO" in New Orleans, Louisiana for three years, I witnessed some exceptional work from the dedicated employees across the Gulf Coast to support long-term recovery. Despite some negative press associated with FEMA's efforts, I saw many successful local stories that never made the national headlines. I guess you could call it "the other side of the storm."

Whenever I would wear my FEMA shirt, many people would come up to me and would extend a handshake and a "thank you" as a FEMA representative. They told stories of the support they received

---

8 John Kotter, "What Leaders Really Do," *Harvard Business Review Leadership Insights*, 2010

DEVELOP YOUR "LEADERSHIP SIGNATURE"

for the temporary living quarters and financial assistance that went to them and their families, or to their schools and communities. A significant number of employees in the workforce were themselves survivors of Hurricane Katrina. Like their neighbors, many of them lost everything to the terrible "storm of the century."

Hiring these people was one means to assist in the local recovery since many of them lost their jobs due to the storm. More importantly, who better to show empathy to an individual or community requiring assistance than people who have been there and walked in their shoes? I thought it was only fair that the top performers assigned to the Recovery Offices should receive a small performance bonus. The problem was that like many issues related to Hurricane Katrina; we were on new ground for many of them. Some in FEMA Headquarters back in Washington, DC were concerned of the potential negative perception of using disaster funds for performance bonuses.

Teaming with the Gulf Coast Administrator in New Orleans, I successfully lobbied for and won *legitimate* approval for funds to pay small bonuses to the best of the best in recognition of their outstanding support. It was the right thing to do.

While at The Citadel, in my Vice President department, we developed a formal recognition program that included Employee of the Quarter and Employee of the Year awards. The winners received a small amount of $50 in their paycheck, a certificate, and their picture professionally taken and prominently displayed on our recognition board in our main hallway. Most important, I announced the winners (always a surprise) at our quarterly "all hands" gathering. More than once, the award recipients were moved to the point of tears when I called them up front of all their peers. That is how powerful the impact of rewards can be. Even a simple "thank you" can make a difference.

Just as a thumb is not the only finger on your hand, using rewards is not the only way to influence. Maintain a good balance among all the power factors. Next, we see how acquiring and sharing knowledge is another important attribute for an aspiring leader.

Index finger: Sharing Knowledge

"In today's environment, hoarding knowledge ultimately erodes your power. If you know something very important, the way to get power is by actually sharing it."[9]

Joseph Badaracco, Harvard Business School Professor

Former Lord Chancellor of England Francis Bacon once said, "Knowledge is power." When someone points with his or her index finger to his or her head, the gesture usually means that the person is thinking hard about an issue, or has come up with a good idea – an "aha" moment. In our case, we use the index finger to represent

---

9   Found at website QuoteSpeak, https://www.quotespeak.com/professional-quotes/business-quotes/best-sharing-knowledge-quotes-inspirational-motivational/4/

that a leader can possess general knowledge that is valuable to the organization. A leader has three objectives when it comes to using knowledge as an element of power and influence:

- Acquire knowledge
- Share the knowledge
- Build trust so that the knowledge is readily received

One of my favorite military assignments involved teaching a leadership course as an adjunct instructor at the Air Force Academy in Colorado Springs, Colorado. This was no easy task. Sitting in the classroom were some of our nation's most capable and brightest individuals. I recall the advice the head of the Department once told me. "You need to always stay ahead of the students."

He explained that an effective instructor could not just follow the course syllabus and go over the assigned readings every class. If that was the case, what *additional value* did you bring into the classroom? The students could do the same thing themselves. The mentor encouraged me to do extra research on my own so that I could do more than just repeat what was in the instructor's guidebook.

Through hard work and preparation, I acquired enough knowledge to stay ahead of my group of students. I got into a habit of reading leadership books and articles, in addition to our formal textbook. The morning that I taught class, I would wake up at 5 a.m. to read the morning newspaper and see if I could use any of the current events to emphasis that day's lesson.

I went further by effectively communicating, or sharing the knowledge, to the students. Whenever possible, I showed movie video clips to drive home a key leadership topic. I invited guest speakers to the classroom to share their own experience and expertise on various lessons. After reading an article about him in the city newspaper, I asked the new chief of the Colorado Springs Fire Department to be a guest speaker on the challenges of leading his department. I even invited Skip, the Airmen who beat me in the day-off challenge in Germany, to be a guest speaker on followership. Both were bit hits.

Finally, I earned the trust of my class through a variety of means. Whether attending their athletic events, becoming a mentor, or just treating them with courtesy and respect, they knew that I had their best interests in mind. Without trust, no matter how much knowledge I had acquired to share with my students, they would not be sufficiently open to receive it.

Not using and sharing knowledge would be like not being able to use your index finger. The following gestures or actions would be limited or impossible without the use of your index finger.

- Making a "We're number one" gesture
- Typing on the keyboard
- Flashing a "peace" or "victory" sign

A leader acquires knowledge through various means, and in doing so, can stay ahead of the group. A leader can obtain knowledge through education, professional certifications, personal experience or experience of others, and from exposure to information received by the nature of the leader's position or perch.

Pursuing the next level of education is important to stay abreast of technology and business practices in your chosen career field and general management techniques.

- If you have just graduated with your Associates Degree, go for your Bachelors.

- If you have finished your Bachelor's Degree, go for your Masters.

When selected as the first and only Chief Financial Officer for Hurricane Katrina recovery efforts in New Orleans, Louisiana, my wife Brenda and I moved from the Washington, DC area to the Gulf Coast. At the time, I was about halfway through an Executive Master's

DEVELOP YOUR "LEADERSHIP SIGNATURE"

in Leadership program at Georgetown University. I thought it only fair to the Recovery Administrator in New Orleans that I focus entirely on our recovery mission, so I temporarily withdrew from my educational pursuit.

After one year, however, I arranged with Georgetown to pick up the Master's program at the point I had left off earlier. This was no easy task to complete. For over four months, every other Friday afternoon, I would wake up at 2 a.m. to drive from Biloxi, Mississippi to the New Orleans airport and catch the earliest possible flight across country to be in class on time at noon. Unlike most of the other students who resided in the DC area, I then had to worry about finding a place to stay during the weekend.

The extra expense of round-trip airfare, rental cars, lodging, and food twice per month was an additional financial burden to manage. In the end, it was all worth the effort. Oftentimes, I would return to work on Monday and put into practice an idea or concept learned from the previous weekend. Pursuing the Georgetown Master's program met my own objective of acquiring knowledge to stay ahead of my group.

Interestingly, General Colin Powell, former Secretary of State and Chairman of the Joint Chiefs of Staff, spoke at a recent Georgetown gathering of MBA students and remarked about the importance of education on his career. He noted that by earning his Master's in Business Administration (MBA) he became a better leader. What he learned around basic human psychology and other people aspects was invaluable to him in future leadership roles.[10]

Although a formal education is an important means to do so, it is by no means the only way.

Pursuing a professional certification is also important to acquire the appropriate depth of knowledge in your career field. In my own case, I obtained a certification as a Certified Government Financial Manager (CGFM) through the Association of Government Accountants

---

10   Former Secretary of State Colin Powell Address "Leadership without Authority", Georgetown McDonough School of Business website, September 27, 2017

(AGA). The certification represents the wide range of knowledge and skills that a professional financial manager needs to succeed at all levels of government.

Another value of pursuing a professional certification is the extensive research and studying of applicable laws, guidance, and policy in your discipline. By obtaining a professional certification, you become an expert in your field.

It is important to recognize to use your newly gained knowledge for the common good, and not in a negative manner. That would be counter-productive. Therefore, one thing a leader should never do is to use your own personal knowledge as a hammer against others when they ask you to share it. Do not be a leader who is too quick to anger, or demonstrate impatience, when a follower is seeking feedback from a leader. I have seen poor leaders who often put a dagger into a needed dialogue. Be careful to stay away from the following statements:

- "I cannot believe you just asked that question."
- "Why in the world would you raise that point?"
- "I already mentioned this before a while back."

As a new leader, you should instead embrace the feedback. If someone returns to you 80 percent understanding of the original message, just deal with the other 20 percent not understood and be done with it. There is no need to berate somebody, start all over with the initial message, and pull someone through a knothole unnecessarily. Chances are, if you do, they will not be coming back to you again for guidance or to seek out your knowledge.

By now, you should see the importance of both acquiring knowledge and sharing it with others. In his book, *The Art of the Leader*, William A. Cohen, noted the following:

"Please note that sharing information with others is exactly opposite of the way that many leaders mistakenly try to lead. These leaders horde information and refuse to share it with anyone. They seem to think that if they keep the information to themselves, they will look smarter than those they want to follow them."[11]

At this point, we could stop here with the importance of using rewards and sharing knowledge. As we move to the next set of fingers representing discipline and authority, we are aiming for that balance across all the powers that will make you an effective leader. From their book, *A Leader's Legacy*, Kouzes and Posner acknowledge the limits of a positive approach and describe times when we must react in a negative manner. They conclude:

"When it comes to leading others, it'd be terrific if we only had to do the things that brought great joy to people's lives and to our own. A tough truth about leading – and one that doesn't get talked about enough – is that sometimes you hurt others and sometimes you get hurt. You can't hit the delete key and eliminate these times from your job. You can't delegate them to others. They come with the territory."[12]

Middle finger: Punish Wisely

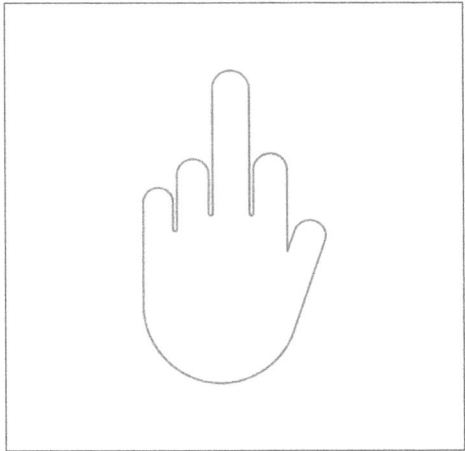

---

11   William Cohen, *The Art of the Leader* (Englewood Cliffs: Prentice Hall, 1990), 65
12   Jim Kouzes and Barry Posner, *A Leader's Legacy* (San Francisco: Jossey-Bass Publishing, 2006), 60

"The superior man is clear-minded and cautious in imposing penalties."

Ancient Chinese Proverb

When I enlisted in the Air Force right out of high school, my first assignment was at Lackland Air Force Base in San Antonio, Texas for basic training. All the Training Instructors were imposing figures, but I remember one. He was big, tall, and mean. This one Sergeant had a habit of getting in your face and lightly poking at your chest with his middle finger. I must admit it felt like a jackhammer beating into my chest mainly because of the dramatic effect of him doing so.

In various cultures, the middle finger represents an obscene gesture. In our case, we use the middle finger to represent the use of discipline or punishment. As we shall discover, the use of this power is perhaps the most complex to use and worth analyzing in more detail.

There is clearly a negative consequence to administering discipline or punishment. As Barbara Deming observed, "Punishment cannot heal spirits, can only break them."[13]

Early in my career as an Air Force officer, I once worked for a Colonel who unfortunately tended to lose his temper, sometimes even in public. On one occasion, I scheduled a meeting directly with the workers involved with a problem area to determine the root cause. There were no supervisors present. I felt that the group would be more likely to speak freely and honestly without their boss in the same room.

The Colonel's office was right next to the conference room where I was conducting the meeting. In the middle of it, his secretary interrupted to say that the Colonel wanted to see me. I informed her that I would do so after the meeting. She indicated that he meant "now" as in immediately. When I walked in to his office, the Colonel was red in the face with anger and began to shout at me that I should never

---

[13] From website Quote HD, http://www.quotehd.com/Quotes/barbara-deming-author-quote-punishment-cannot-heal-spirits-can-only-break

conduct a meeting without the supervisor in the room. He berated me for about fifteen minutes. In this case, the Colonel used the wrong set of power and influence at his disposal. He should have used the situation as a teaching moment. As an experienced and high-ranking officer, he could have shared his knowledge and explain his rationale behind his advice. If he wanted to emphasize his point by being firm, that would be okay too.

However, there was no sharing of knowledge by a seasoned Colonel to a young Lieutenant willing to listen and learn. In reflection, I even see his point about honoring the chain-of-command in the same manner that I expected it from my own staff. When I left the room, however, I only remembered one thing – my boss acting mad and yelling and not much beyond that. In short, the Colonel used the wrong finger – middle (punishment) instead of his index finger (sharing knowledge).

Conversely, the other perspective worth considering is that a leader can do damage by choosing to *not* discipline when the situation calls for it. Just as a child needs boundaries, an organization needs them too. If unacceptable behavior goes unchecked, you are only creating confusion and poor morale in the workplace.

You may be a bit gun shy after reading the negative consequences of choosing to punish perhaps too quickly, and the ramifications if you choose not to. I offer a tool that I developed that may be useful as you start your post-college graduation career – the Beyond A Reasonable Doubt or BARD discipline rule. Most of you are familiar with the legal term, beyond a reasonable doubt. A judge advises jury members to hear and weigh the evidence and reach a conclusion of not guilty or guilty that is beyond a reasonable doubt. The standard is a high one. You can use the Beyond A Reasonable Doubt (BARD) discipline rule as a simple, yet powerful guide in determining when to discipline. The rule goes like this:

Never discipline your people unless you are beyond a reasonable doubt they deserve it

The BARD discipline rule accomplishes two very important outcomes.
- You keep your credibility high by not overreacting too quickly
- When the evidence warrants it, you have no choice but to act

After weighing all the circumstances, if you decide that someone is beyond a reasonable doubt in requiring discipline, you still must be careful not to go overboard in the punishment itself. The punishment should fit the discretion involved.

When deployed for six months in the Middle East, I used the BARD discipline rule on one of my favorite troops. "Nick" was a sharp Non-Commissioned Officer (NCO) with a great attitude, and he worked hard and effectively in our office. During a short time, however, he abused the privilege of a weekly personal phone call to stay in touch with those back home. He also lost the office key that each of us had been issued upon arrival. You might be asking yourself, "What is the big deal? It is only a key and a phone call?"

In the deployment situation, we look forward to our one phone call every week that we could make back to the United States. To be fair to everyone on the installation, we were instructed to keep our calls to 15 minutes. Sure, sometimes we occasionally busted the time by a minute or two, but Nick had done so too many times and way beyond reasonable timelines. In addition, by losing his office key, he placed our own personal safety at risk.

Only a few years earlier, 19 U. S. Air Force members and one Saudi employee were killed because of a terrorist bombing at the Khobar Towers housing complex in Saudi Arabia. Additionally, nearly 400 people of other nationalities were wounded. To improve our Force Protection, the 4404th Provisional Wing relocated to Prince Sultan Air Base, Saudi Arabia. Because of our history with terrorism, losing an office key was considered a breach to safety and security.

I was upset with Nick for putting his teammates at a security risk for carelessness on his part. In addition, by abusing his phone privileges, the commander could have made an example out of our entire unit and we all could have lost our ability to stay in touch with family back home.

I drafted up a letter of admonishment and had Nick formally report in to me with the ranking NCO also present. He stood at attention while I slowly read him the punishment. He signed the letter and readily acknowledged his mistake. If he failed again on either count, the next set of consequences would escalate proportionately. A day or two later, Nick came by and asked me if it would be okay to use the same letter as an example of discipline when he needed to impose it on others. You see, Nick was aspiring to become an officer himself and he knew the value of fair and evenhanded discipline. He was given me feedback that my punishment was the right call and in the right manner.

I stayed in touch with Nick for years after the deployment and I am proud to report that Nick became an outstanding Air Force Intelligence Officer serving his country with distinction.

Part of being a good leader is discernment in making tough decisions involving people. The real value of using the BARD discipline rule is that it keeps your actions consistent. You should not discipline your people merely because you are having a bad day or have a temper problem. The BARD rule in effect slows you down and forces you to catch your breath first. At the same time, the BARD rule also moves you to take decisive action when there is a need to do so. Just because I liked Nick as a person, did not prevent me from disciplining him when appropriate. The BARD discipline rule is a valuable tool for you to use in your future leadership role.

Ring finger: Using your Status and Authority

By earning your new college degree, you are in a better position to move up the career ladder. We use the ring finger to represent that a leader possesses authority by their position or title obtained. During my time at The Citadel, The Military College of South Carolina, the concept of the ring finger demonstrating new status or authority was vividly demonstrated.

Every year, cadets become eligible to wear the cherished class ring upon entering the fall semester before graduation (normally seniors). The graduating year (for example, 19 for the class of 2019) is worn facing *towards* the cadet. Only at the graduation ceremony, can they turn the ring around, so the year faces out, a symbol that they joined the proud ranks of alumni.

On October 11, 2017, my former boss Lt. General John W. Rosa Jr., the 19th President of The Citadel spoke to the class of 2018 at the ring ceremony. He acknowledged the journey they had taken to this point. From matriculation day as a freshman, through the demands imposed at a military college, including physical and mental. Obtaining the ring was a significant milestone. General Rosa reminded the cadets that the ring demonstrates a commitment to conduct themselves as principled leaders. They were to be examples to the lower-class cadets, always following the college's core values of Duty, Honor, and Respect. Upon graduation, the way they behave and the way they treated others represents all alumni.

Soon, you will start (or continue) your climb up the career ladder. It is through *authority* that a manager can issue rewards, or if necessary, administer punishment as discussed in the previous sections. A wise leader uses authority judiciously, not overemphasizing it as the *only* form of influence. In other words, you can't always use the phrase "…because I told you so" with the people you lead. At the same time, a leader should not give away his or authority, because doing so only diminishes their ability to influence others.

A new leader should have three objectives when it comes to authority:

DEVELOP YOUR "LEADERSHIP SIGNATURE"

- Use for benefit of the organization and others
- To draw the line for inappropriate behavior
- Not give away too easily

In the military, a change-of-command ceremony is a special event where the organization gathers to bid farewell to an outgoing commander and welcome onboard a new one. The ceremony is steep in military tradition. I was fortunate to not only attend many of these ceremonies as a spectator, but on two occasions, as an active participant as a new commander. Assuming command, with all its inherent responsibility and authority, is a special moment in a person's career.

During many of the ceremonies, an installation chaplain is part of the event. Many times, the following words were used from Luke 12:48: "For everyone to whom much is given, of him shall much be required." What is required is to use authority for the benefit of the organization and the people within it.

While assigned to Ramstein Air Base in Germany as the Accounting and Finance Officer, I provided career opportunities for numerous enlisted persons. One example that stands out is with a young Staff Sergeant named Gayle. She was sharp in uniform, knowledgeable, and an excellent Non-Commissioned Officer (NCO). One day, she received news that she had been promoted to the next rank, Technical Sergeant (E-6). In the Air Force, when promoted, you receive a line number. The persons that had been in the service the longest were promoted first and so on. Since Gayle was so junior compared to the others, it would take about six months before she would pin on her new stripes.

I spoke with our Superintendent, a Chief Master Sergeant, and together we planned what new responsibilities Gayle would assume when she pinned on the Technical Sergeant stripes. My thoughts were that "getting promoted should mean something." I wanted others in the unit to see that when Gayle reached her personal milestone, there should be a visible change. To continue doing the same job she had as a Staff Sergeant would be inappropriate in my mind.

One of the most important areas to me is customer service. At the largest air base in Europe, our customer service area supported approximately 10,000 military personnel assigned to the installation. How people gauged our entire 150-person Accounting and Finance Office, in both performance and reputation, often went the way of the customer service function.

After consulting with the Chief, we decided that the day Gayle pinned on Technical Sergeant, would be the day she officially took responsibility as the NCO in charge of the Customer Service unit. At a relatively junior rank, she would be responsible for supporting the largest number of customers in the Air Force for someone in her military grade.

When we told Gayle of our plan, she was a bit surprised, and somewhat apprehensive. She knew firsthand the importance of the customer service function to both our office and the entire base. If things bogged down, everybody from pilots who needed to be in the air, to headquarters staff with oversight of the entire European theater, would feel the impact.

In the days and weeks leading up to the big day, we encouraged Gayle with positive reinforcement. In hindsight, it was a risky move on my part because I oversaw the entire Finance operation and I was entrusting a key part of it to relatively junior person. Yet, this opportunity could mean a lot for Gayle down the road. It came as no surprise that Gayle did perform as expected. She took advantage of her big break and went on to become a Chief Master Sergeant in her own right years later, the highest enlisted rank possible.

As a new leader, you also need to emphasize certain non-negotiable lines in the sand early and often. Clearly and forcefully, spell out a zero tolerance for any discrimination or sexual harassment. Continue to re-draw those lines because over time they can become less clear. By drawing a line in the sand for discrimination and harassment, hopefully you minimize the occasions when you need to use discipline when someone crosses the line.

Finally, a leader should not give away their authority too easily. I retired from the United States Air Force after 28 years' service that included eight years as an enlisted person. Earning my commission was no easy task as I worked a part-time job, served as a non-commissioned officer, and had a family that required my attention. At night, I took as many as three classes per semester towards a bachelor's degree that enabled me to eventually become an officer. Even though I was proud of my achievement, I did not feel I deserved any special treatment because of it. At the same time, I was not going to tolerate when I thought someone was not giving me the proper respect to my hard-earned authority. I developed a rule that helped guide me in this respect for years to come when it came to authority.

I do not want any special treatment or more respect given to me for my accomplishments, but I also do not deserve any less respect either.

Pinky finger: Using Relationships

> "Technology has given us the ability to reach out over great distances and control actions and people in ways that leaders even fifty years ago could never imagine. But today we have a saying: high tech, low touch. The more technology mediates our communications and contacts, the less personal our relationships."[14]
>
> *Tony Zinni, from his book Leading the Charge*

When someone refers to being wrapped around your finger (normally the pinky), the impression is usually of a close personal relationship. If two people intertwine their two pinky fingers, it is commonly referred to as a "pinky shake." Younger people often use their pinky fingers to go along with a "pinky swear." Implying to keep a solemn promise between two friends. Fittingly, the pinky finger anchors our leadership signature concept. We started with two positive influence factors, the thumb (using rewards) and the index finger (sharing knowledge). The next two fingers, middle and ring finger, represented somewhat tougher forms of influence by using punishment and authority.

The pinky finger, therefore, nicely rounds out the forms of influence a leader can possess, since the pinky finger represents a leader forging a relationship with those around him or her. In her book, *Playbook for Success*, former basketball player and coach Nancy Lieberman offered sound advice to form a relationship with others. The Hall-of-Famer and motivation speaker and author noted the following:

"You have to have social skills. If you're working in an office and you ride up the elevator with someone, ask how he or she is. Try to remember people's names. Even if you don't really care, fake it. I know the impression it leaves on me when someone remembers to ask about TJ or my mom. Simple acts of kindness like these are

---

[14] Tony Zinni and Tony Koltz, *Leading the Charge: Leadership Lessons from the Battlefield to the Boardroom* (New York: Palgrave MacMillan, 2009)

important to building strength and cohesion on your team."[15]

There are numerous ways to forge a good relationship with people, to include the following:

- Communicate often
- Use your Emotional Intelligence (EQ)
- Have fun at work

Communicate often

To establish a personal relationship with others, you must communicate with them on a regular basis. For many assignments, I led large groups of people, up to 150 in one overseas tour. Almost daily, I started the day by walking around the office to at least greet the staff and make a quick personal connection. A leader must be seen (and heard) often.

What you communicate is also important. I believe that probing about outside interests is important and should occur on a regular basis. However, another purpose of the regular walk-around is to *take your office to them*. You often hear that someone has an *open-door policy*. How many times will someone ever jump his or her chain-of-command and seek out the boss on a matter? Probably, likely, very infrequently. When you walk around your organization, you *enable* that type of communication to occur. Many times, by being just present, my followers would stop to ask me about a rumor or hot issue. This was my opportunity to provide what was really going on. Perhaps it was to seek my advice on an issue. It did not matter, by being present, I was in a better position to communicate.

Use your Emotional Intelligence (EQ)

Your ability to assess people's feelings is also important to a leader. Daniel Goleman is a pioneer in the Emotional Intelligence (EQ)

---

15 Nancy Lieberman, *Playbook for Success: A Hall of Famer's Business Tactics for Teamwork and Leadership* (Hoboken: John Wiley and Sons Publishing, 2010), 108

research and teachings. He and his colleagues attempted to examine the relationship between EQ and leadership performance in the workplace. Objective criteria included profitability of the organization they led. The results were striking.[16]

When Goleman calculated the ingredients of excellent performance such as a person's technical skills, intelligence (IQ), and emotional intelligence (EQ), it was EQ that proved twice as important as the other two. As Goleman explained, "It was once thought that the components of emotional intelligence were 'nice to have' in business leaders. But now we know that, for the sake of performance, these are ingredients that leaders 'need to have'."[17]

The five components of emotional intelligence and some of the hallmarks for each include the following:[18]

- Self-awareness (self-confidence but self-deprecating sense of humor)
- Self-regulation (trustworthiness and integrity)
- Motivation (optimism, strong desire to achieve)
- Empathy (cross-cultural sensitivity)
- Social skill (expert in building teams and leading change)

In the end, whereas IQ can help you read a book, EQ can help you when you are trying to read (and lead) people. Both are important but possessing and using EQ can take a leader a long way.

Have fun at work

I must admit, I cannot think of a day at work that I did not laugh at least once. Laughing reduces stress, gets our blood flowing, and combats fatigue and boredom. I even found a way to use it in the classroom at the highly-disciplined Air Force Academy.

Although an Adjunct Instructor for the Department of Behavioral

---

16 Daniel Goleman, "What Makes a Leader?" *Harvard Business Review* (Leadership Insights Collection, 2010), 36
17 Ibid.
18 Ibid.

Sciences, my primary duties were in the Office of Admissions. Cindy, our Administrative Assistant, would often ask about the class I taught so I arranged for her to join me the next morning. By coincidence, that day would be on April 1st, or April Fool's Day.

We plotted our strategy. Cindy would pose as a classroom evaluator for the Dean of the Faculty. She found an old briefcase in the storage closet that looked like something out of the 1960s. It was plain, bulky, and a bit torn. It was ideal for our prank. It was also large enough to hold a dozen donuts and a container of orange juice that I occasionally snuck into the classroom as a treat for the students.

The next morning, Cindy dressed for the scheme perfectly, wearing very conservative clothing, glasses, and little make-up. As we entered the classroom, Cindy carrying the briefcase, found a seat in the back of the classroom. "Class, we have a visitor today," I announced. "Miss Cindy Jones is an evaluator for the Dean, who personally chose her to provide an assessment on randomly selected instructors. So just be yourselves and pretend that she is not here." Cindy brought out a notepad and pen to begin taking notes for her "evaluation."

Sometimes, I would begin the class with one of David Letterman's "Top 10 lists." They were corny but the cadets always got a kick out of them and burst out laughing. For this day, I chose the best material: A Top 10 list of how college athletes cheat in the classroom. My class had several varsity athletes by the way. I began reading through the list, pausing for effect after each one.

The cadets had no idea what to do! Since I told them to be themselves, should they laugh at the silly jokes? On the other hand, because the evaluator was in the room, should they *not* laugh because she might perceive it as improper classroom protocol? The cadets played it safe and chose the latter – to sit quietly.

Cindy, meanwhile, was acting up a storm. She would shake her head in disgust, mumble something, and then write furiously on her notepad. The cadets kept looking at me, the projector screen, and then over to the "evaluator." Cindy later told me that she could barely contain from not laughing herself.

Finally, after one of her snide comments beneath her breath, I asked her if anything was wrong. We began improvising at this point. Cindy informed me that this was not what she expected and that the Dean (a General Officer) would not be very pleased when she reported to him. I told her that this was still my classroom and I would instruct the way I wanted to. If she did not like it, she was welcome to leave. She picked up her notepad and stormed out of the classroom, leaving the briefcase behind. "We will see about this," her parting remarks out the door.

The cadets' eyes were as big as saucers, and they were speechless. Finally, one cadet asked, "Sir, are you going to be in trouble?" I continued fussing about the need for an evaluator in the first place and headed towards the briefcase left behind. I opened it and after a few moments of looking through the case, brought out the donuts and the orange juice.

When the cadets let out an audible sigh of relief, Cindy stepped back in the classroom after waiting quietly outside and gave a hearty "April Fool's!" She stayed and helped to pass out the refreshments as we continued with our normal classroom discussion.

As new graduates, and future leaders, you will need to establish your own management style. You may even get advice to be a strict boss, where a leader does not need to establish a relationship of any kind with their followers.

In this thought process, a leader's authority is enough to propel others toward the desired outcome. My experience is vastly different. As Kouzes and Posner noted in their book, *A Leader's Legacy*, "We will work harder and more effectively for people we like. And we like them in direct proportion to how they make us feel."[19]

Leaders who try to figure out ways to establish and build a relationship with their people probably *do work harder*. I also believe, however, that others will want to work much *harder for them*.

---

19 Jim Kouzes and Barry Posner, *A Leader's Legacy* (San Francisco: Jossey-Bass Publishing, 2006)

DEVELOP YOUR "LEADERSHIP SIGNATURE"

Putting it all together: The Love You hand gesture leadership tip

The American Sign Language sign for "I love you" is the thumb, index, and pinky fingers pointing out and the two middle fingers held back. This gesture is an ideal means to now show how and when the five available powers should be used. Sometimes showing love includes "tough love" when appropriate and necessary.

My military experience concluded with being a squadron commander at an Air Force base in Mississippi. On a professional level, serving as a commander is a role all officers strive to attain. As actor Samuel L. Jackson, playing a Marine Colonel in the movie, *Rules of Engagement*, said, "There is no greater honor an American can have then to command." He was right. Essentially, when given the command, you receive the authority and responsibility for accomplishing both the assigned mission while caring for the people in your charge.

Only a commander is authorized to administer serious punishment according to the Uniform Code of Military Justice.

WHEN THE CAP FALLS

During my tour as squadron commander, I tried to make the workplace more enjoyable and foster a rewarding environment to work in. One Halloween day I encouraged people to dress up in costume (I wore an orange prisoner suit) and we walked over to the child daycare center to have fun with the kids in our costumes. At one office holiday party, I organized a small group of us to dance at the gathering. We were not very good, but the audience got a kick out of our antics.

During this time period, our youngest enlisted member (let's call him "Jim") got into some trouble that involved alcohol. He was a fine young man and I felt a special fondness for him, as he was a solid performer, a bit reserved, and always polite and courteous. When I got a call that Jim had been in a fight in the dormitory, there was no wiggle room to let it go. Recall the Beyond a Reasonable Doubt or BARD rule that called for discipline when warranted. I could not tolerate his unacceptable behavior, so I administered the necessary punishment swiftly and appropriately.

Only a few months later, the squadron along with the rest of the organizations on base, would undergo a rigorous Operational Readiness Inspection. The command headquarters from Texas would send a team of professionals to evaluate mission readiness over a demanding week-long review. We had been preparing for the inspection for about six months as it was an important event. I also did not want to disappoint my boss, the General Officer in charge of the installation, since the inspection was a report card on his performance.

As we neared the last week before the Inspector General (IG) visit, I still needed to make one important decision. Who would deliver the important orientation briefing to the IG staff when they arrived on the first day of the inspection?

The orientation briefing was important for several reasons. It was an opportunity to establish a good first impression on the visitors. Earlier in my career, I learned that lesson when the orientation session did not go well, and it set the tone for a less than optimal review and

DEVELOP YOUR "LEADERSHIP SIGNATURE"

report. Missing your mark leaves a negative impression that is hard to overcome. Second, the orientation briefing was a means to highlight our achievements of the past several years and leave a positive image with the IG staff.

In many cases, the squadron commander is the one who gives the mission orientation since the inspection team is evaluating his or her unit. Other times, a commander may designate the briefing to a company grade officer such as a Captain or First Lieutenant. After thinking about the options, I decided to go a very different route. I would choose the most junior enlisted person in the 75-person squadron to give the important IG orientation briefing. That person happened to be Jim, the enlisted man who only a few months ago I punished for his drinking and disorderly incident.

When I informed Jim of my decision, he at first was a bit hesitant. He had not faced such a daunting challenge before in his short military career. I encouraged Jim that he would represent our unit with distinction and that we would be with him every step of the way.

When the big day came, we gathered in our large conference room to welcome the visiting IG staff to our squadron. As I walked up to the front of the room, I made just a few opening remarks. The inspectors seemed surprised when I then introduced Jim to proceed with the presentation while I sat down. For about 30 minutes Jim maneuvered through all the slides without a hitch. In fact, he had nailed the briefing. A few days later during the inspection, the senior IG official told me that he had never seen such a move by a squadron commander. He was impressed that I had chosen the most junior person to give the important first day orientation. I never told him how significant it was considering Jim's circumstance only a few weeks earlier. In the end, we received an overall Excellent rating that helped our overall installation rating as well.

By grouping the fingers into one of two categories (positive or less positive), we can see which influence factors should be used more proactively and which ones a leader should be more reactive in their use. See fig 1.

Positive Factors – Be Proactive (fingers out)		
Finger	**Type of power**	**Visual**
Thumb	Rewards	
Index	Knowledge	
Pinky	Relationships	
Less Positive Factors – Be More Reactive (fingers in)		
Finger	**Type of power**	**Visual**
Middle	Punishment	

DEVELOP YOUR "LEADERSHIP SIGNATURE"

Ring	Authority	
	Factors Combined	**Visual**
I love you hand gesture		

Figure 1

In their excellent book, *The Great Workplace: How to Build it, How to Keep it, and Why it Matters*, authors Michael Burchell and Jennifer Robin, search for what makes organizations special. In one example, Rob Burton of Hoar Construction shared the following: "When it comes to specific issues, I think one of the biggest mistakes that CEOs make is to look forward to the power and authority that they're given. My advice is, sure that's true, but take that and put it in your pocket because you don't need to use it. When you need to use it, it's there and everybody knows that. You can so no when you want to. The better thing to do is to forget about it and stay humble and go to work with your friends and get the job done. That's been my philosophy about it. It's not an ego trip. It's a lifestyle."[20]

---

20 Michael Burchel and Jennifer Robin, *The Great Workplace: How to Build It, How to Keep It, and Why It Matters* (San Francisco: Jossey-Bass Publishing, 2011), 206-207.

When to be Proactive as a Leader

Although all our five power factors are important, a leader should be more forward leaning in three of them.

- Promoting the use of rewards (thumb)
- Sharing knowledge (index finger)
- Forging relationships (pinky)

The reason you must be proactive in these areas is it will take an effort on your part to ensure that they happen. For example, developing and maintaining a robust rewards program requires a commitment of time and resources. The same holds true for acquiring and sharing knowledge with others, whether through continued education or certifications to "stay ahead of the group." Finally, it takes a positive effort to forge a relationship with others. Saying "hi" to someone is not going to cut it. Being proactive means consciously pursuing these objectives daily.

When to be Reactive as a Leader

If it is best to be proactive in the three powers and influence factors represented by the thumb, index finger, and the pinky, then logically we would be more selective in use of the other two;

- Using authority (ring finger)
- Punish when the line is crossed (middle finger)

There are times when a leader should use power to push the use of mainly positive factors such as rewards, knowledge, or to build a relationship. There will be other times, however, when a leader should exert authority or administer punishment. In his book, *100 Ways to Motivate Others*, Steve Chandler calls on a leader to be a "Bad Cop" on occasion. This means having direct conversations to a subordinate who is failing that is something like this, "I believe in you. I know what you can do. When you don't do it, you let yourself and the team down. I won't allow that. Time to wake up."[21]

Chandler goes on to suggest that Bad Cop tactics, in our case the use of punishment or exerting our authority, is best used only when you need to do so. "Obviously, you don't call on Bad Cop every day. Only after every Good Cop approach is exhausted. But Bad Cop can be a great wake-up call for someone who has never been challenged in life to be the best she can be. And once the Bad Cop session is over, and the person is back in the game, giving it a good effort, bring Good Cop back right away to complete the process."[22]

In our love you-type gesture, you bring out the middle and ring finger in reaction to an event that you cannot choose to let go. These two middle fingers are tucked in since they are not normally used while the other three are fully exposed and ready to be used robustly.

Be an upbeat leader until the time calls for you to be otherwise.

Reevaluating the Leadership Signature Test

We are now in a good position to again look at the signature test we took to start this chapter. I asked my wife Brenda to do the signature test with three signatures. The first signature used only two fingers and represent the tough boss approach since only discipline and authority powers are used. This is by far the worst signature. In the same manner, you would be a marginal leader if using only negative influence. The second signature reflects Brenda's signature when only three fingers are used, representing the likeable boss approach of promoting only rewards, knowledge, and building personal relationships. It is noticeably better than the first signature, however, it is not the optimal one. The third and final signature reflects Brenda's signature when all five fingers are used, representing the complete and balanced boss approach. It reflects signature 1 plus signature 2. All three signatures are shown at figure 2.

---

21 Steve Chandler, *100 Ways to Motivate Others: How Great Leaders Can Produce Insane Results Without Driving People Crazy* (Franklin Lakes: Career Press, 2008), 79.
22 Ibid.

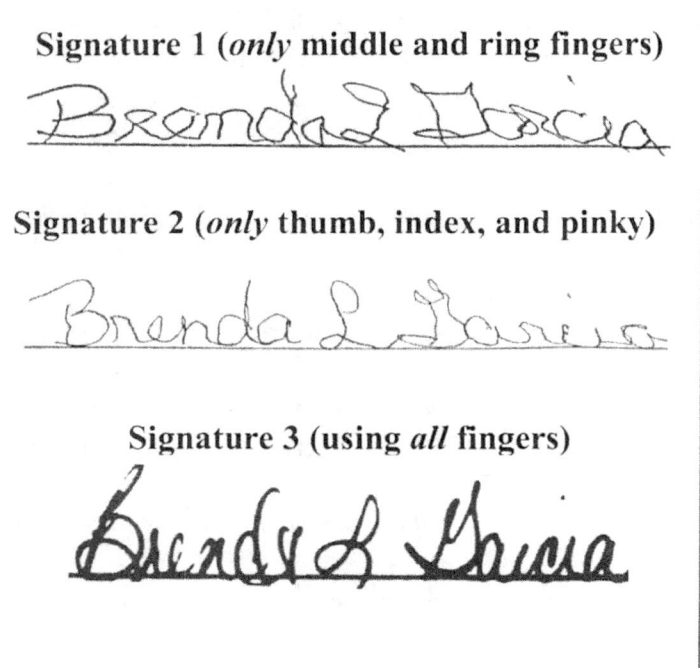

Figure 2

Final thoughts on the Leadership Signature principle

I believe the key to your success as a new graduate entering the work force is to have leadership balance. The I Love You gesture provides us that balance by reminding us that although a leader possesses a wide range of influence factors, using the appropriate one at the appropriate time is essential. It is not one set (positive/proactive) or the other (negative/reactive); it is using *both* in a balanced fashion.

I encourage you to work on your own leadership signature, and my hope is that it always reflects the fullest repertoire of power and influence as a leader. Doing so will benefit you, the people you serve with, and help contribute to your organization's success.

CHAPTER 3

A good leader should LISTEN

"I am rather inclined to silence."

President Abraham Lincoln

ONE OF THE highest rated lessons from my leadership course taught at The Citadel surprised me. It was on the importance of listening. The positive student feedback surprised me because I thought it was a rather routine lesson that while I considered important enough to include in the syllabus, did not expect such good results. To be somewhat immodest, many of my other lessons were original concepts that the students had never heard of before. But listening? We do that every day.

That was the point that I discovered with this lesson and why we include it as an important principle for new graduates. Although we all listen, we often do so only halfheartedly. We may hear words spoken, but we do not listen for the meaning *behind* the words. There is a big difference. As mentioned in the last chapter, whereas IQ can help you read a book, emotional intelligence or EQ can help you when you are trying to read (and lead) people.

There are several key aspects to effective listening:

- Why we should listen
- Barriers to why we do not listen
- How to listen effectively
- Upon listening, when to act

Why we should listen

What most people look for in any leader is mutual respect between both parties. Showing respect comes from listening. As Bryant McGill observed, "One of the most sincere forms of respect is actually listening to what another has to say."[23]

Active listening means we are paying close attention to what the other person has to say by giving our undivided attention. That demonstrates respect.

As a new graduate and future leader, when someone comes to you with a problem or a suggestion, to keep your head down while on your cell phone will most certainly stop the feedback loop. You may miss important information that is valuable to you.

In his book, *You can't lead with your feet on the desk*, Ed Duller, President of Marriott Lodging International, had this to say about the importance of listening.

> "if you're like me, you become impatient with too much chatter. Yet the failure to listen carefully to others is a serious mistake. Aside from showing a lack of respect, thereby damaging whatever relationship you have to begin with, the information you miss can prove costly."[24]

That will also go for not only your followers, but perhaps more importantly, the larger circle of people that you will interact with as you start your new career, as shown at figure 3.

---

23 From website Brainy Quote, https://www.brainyquote.com/quotes/bryant_h_mcgill_168254
24 Ed Duller, *You Can't Lead With Your Feet On the Desk: Building Relationships, Breaking Down Barriers, and Delivering Profits* (Hoboken: John Wiley and Sons Publishing, 2010), 115.

A GOOD LEADER SHOULD LISTEN

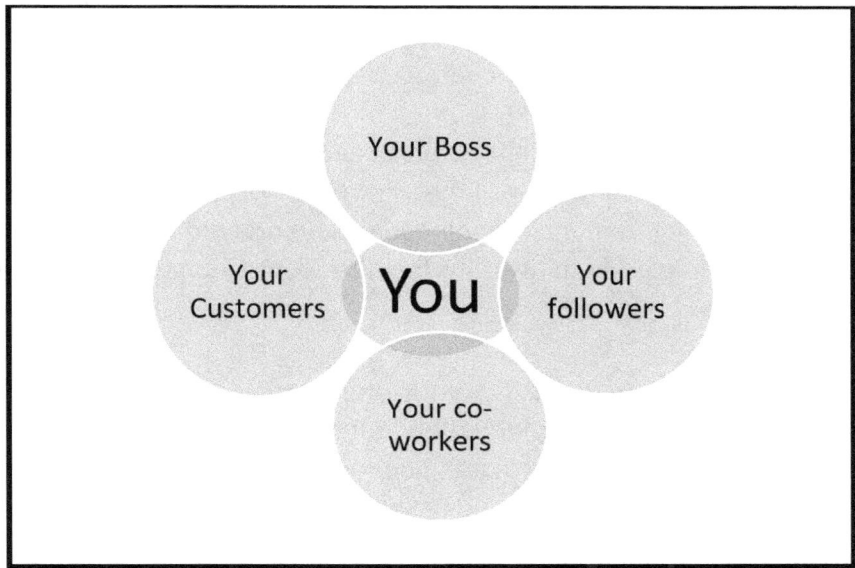

Figure 3

If effective listening allows a leader to demonstrate respect to others, and enables you to gather necessary feedback from various levels of people we interact with, why then do we not properly listen?

Barriers to why we do not listen

"I like to listen. I have learned a great deal from listening carefully. Most people never listen."

Ernest Hemingway, Journalist

Throughout my career, it would be fair to say that I am probably one of the quieter persons compared to my peers at an organizational meeting. Yet, I would also consider myself one of the most engaged at the boardroom table. Why? Because I am taking in what is being said and looking for the larger meaning of the discussion. In my mind, I am strategically connecting the various dots across the landscape.

When necessary, I will speak up to validate or contradict a point.

Winston Churchill got it right when he said, "Courage is what it takes to stand up and speak; courage is also what it takes to sit down and listen."[25]

We often do not listen effectively because of our own ego. We filter out what people are saying because we are not open to other ideas beyond our own. This is close-mindedness. In order to properly listen to others, we need humility. Our first President George Washington demonstrated both traits.

> "When Washington first went to the Virginia legislature, he was known for being incredibly quiet – he hardly uttered a word. He became known as a good listener, however, as well as a thoughtful and judicious thinker, all because he put into practice another of his strongest leadership traits – humility. Throughout his life, in fact, Washington listened far more than he talked."[26]

We will spend an entire chapter on managing your ego later in the book. Another barrier to listening besides our ego is thinking we must speak up to demonstrate our value. As a new college graduate, consider the quality of your words instead of the quantity.

Another barrier that prevents effective listening is a physical one, the space between others and us. In my office, I set up a small table as a place to talk with someone for a scheduled meeting or even a drop-in visit. This means I get up from behind my desk and walk over to the table. Unlike a previous boss I worked for, I do not believe a conversation can occur while I remain at my desk or facing my computer screen. If anything, I bring only a notepad and pen to capture

---

25 Found at website, Brainy Quote, https://www.brainyquote.com/quotes/winston_churchill_161628
26 James Rees and Stephen Spignesi, *George Washington's Leadership Lessons: What the Father of our Country Can Teach Us About Effective Leadership and Character* (Hoboken: John Wiley and Sons, Inc, 2007), 97

any takeaways from the dialogue.

Now that we have reviewed why we should listen, and some of the barriers that prevent us from doing so, we can move to how best to listen.

How to listen effectively

A right answer is good, a right question is better.

Whether in front of my students in my leadership classes, or in one of my staff meetings, I considered it a successful outcome when there was an exchange of ideas. If I did all the talking, good communication did not occur. The root words associated with communication include to share, impart, join, unite, and to participate in.

To keep a dialogue going, I was cautious not to provide an immediate answer to a question or problem. "What do you think?" can be one of the more powerful four words you will ever use as a new graduate in the workplace. Whether in my classroom or office meetings, I tried to give others a chance to speak who were not prone to do so. Asking them how they felt allowed a more diverse set of viewpoints.

In their book, *Judgment: How Winning Leaders Make Great Calls*, Noel Tichy and Warren Bennis write how Jack Welch, former CEO of General Electric, would engage his younger managers in an interactive give-and-take mutual learning session. Welch would actively solicit their opinions and ask them how they would solve a problem.[27]

Leadership author John Maxwell captured it right when he noted that the four most important words regarding listening are, "What is your opinion?"[28]

In addition to asking questions, in her *Harvard Business Review*

---

27 Noel Tichy and Warren Bennis, *Judgment: How Winning Leaders Make Great Calls* (New York: The Penguin Group, 2007), 239-240.
28 John Maxwell, *Be a People Person: Effective Leadership Through Effective Relationships* (Colorado Springs: David Cook, 2007), 29.

article entitled, "Listening Is an Overlooked Leadership Tool." Melissa Daimler suggests other tips for better ways to listen.[29]

Look people in the eye

We need to make eye contact to effectively listen to another person. This means removing obstacles, some already mentioned, such as cell phones or other electronic devices. Looking people directly in the eyes allows you to pick up non-verbal signals that you might otherwise miss.[30]

Create space in your day

Another important idea is to leave space on your daily calendar so that you have time for reflection and more energy for conversations. This will take a conscious effort on your part and delegation to involve others. Having a full calendar every day is not always the sign of your importance. Allowing time to think and interact with others is a necessity.[31]

Gus Pagonis, an Army lieutenant general (three-star), validates Daimler's tips to improve listening. In his case, it started with seeking constructive feedback from his staff. To his surprise, being a better listener was one of the first suggestions to improve. That is a common problem as we *think* we are good listeners, but in reality, most of us could be better at it.

To the general's credit, he sought more specific feedback on what he was doing wrong (or could be better at) when it came to effective listening. Here is what he discovered that a new graduate can benefit from a senior leader's perspective:[32]

---

29 Melissa Daimler, "Listening is an Overlooked Leadership Tool," *Harvard Business Review*, May 25, 2016
30 Ibid.
31 Ibid.
32 Gus Pagonis, "Leadership in a Combat Zone," *Harvard Business Review*, December 2001

- Watch your body language. General Pagonis reinforces the earlier advice to maintain eye contact with others while they are speaking and avoid appearing distracted by doing other tasks.

- Push routine paperwork to later in the day to allow more time for others to talk uninterrupted.

- Mentor advice, "Never pass up the opportunity to remain silent."

As a result of his actions to improve, the constructive feedback paid off. Instead of listening skills being perceived as a weakness, it eventually became a strength.

When to act

Another key aspect of effective listening is to when to act, especially when receiving feedback from followers. As an emerging leader, you may feel that you should charge ahead with a decision upon listening to input from others. In some cases, that might be true. More often, it is okay to process the information and not overreact. When I was a young Captain in the Air Force, I had the privilege of leading a 100-person organization in Wichita Falls, Texas. It was my first real leadership responsibility where I was not a Deputy, supporting the person who was ultimately in charge. I reported to a full Colonel who had oversight of the entire organization.

On occasion, I would drop by the Colonel's office to share how things were going in my branch. Being an optimist, I normally focused on the good events happening, as my staff gave me many positive actions to report. However, there were times when I also shared some of the natural challenges that occur in leadership. Rather than just listening, and letting me vent a bit, my supervisor was too quick to try to solve my problem! If an issue involved an external organization, he would literally pick up the phone to call other Colonels and begin to act at his level.

While I appreciated his support and willingness to help, if I really needed his involvement, I would have asked for it. Followers need a safe place to let off some steam. As a boss, you can quietly listen, and offer encouragement and reassurance. Towards the end of the conversation, only then you should ask the specific question, "What can I do to help?" If your follower takes you up on your offer, then engage to seek a resolution to the problem. Many times, like I did with my Colonel, I would merely state that was not necessary.

Good Leaders LISTEN

Years ago, I developed an acronym that helps me always remember the importance of being a good listener and what happens when we are. Hopefully, it captures what we've learned in this short chapter in an easy-to-remember form.

When we LISTEN, positive things happen, to include:

> **L**earn from others
> **I**nstill pride of ownership
> **S**hare the center stage
> **T**eamwork promoted
> **E**go kept in check
> **N**ew ideas created

By combining all these elements in one paragraph, you can see why you should always strive to be a leader who listens.

> A good leader Learns from others while Instilling pride of ownership by Sharing the center stage with others so that Teamwork is promoted through keeping one's Ego in check to allow New ideas to be created.

The principle of effective listening will be especially valuable to you as you begin your career after graduation. A good leader does not always mean needing to be out in front of everybody else. If you are too far ahead, you are not close enough to hear and listen to what others are trying to tell you.

CHAPTER 4

Climb the Leader's Pyramid (for balance and consistency)

> "The greatest manager of all time was the man who conceived, designed, and built – totally unprecedented – the first pyramid...no manager I am in knowledge of could possibly accomplish what this fellow did."[33]
>
> *Dr. Peter Drucker, management guru*

The Leader's Pyramid concept has allowed me to meet extraordinary mission requirements in extraordinary places. From my time in New Orleans as the "Katrina CFO" after the storm, to my deployment in the desert of Saudi Arabia during Operation Southern Watch, the Leader's Pyramid kept my actions balanced and consistent.

Interestingly, this principle developed in a classroom at the United States Air Force Academy while teaching a leadership course. During that time, I had shared with the students my "put yourself third" belief that a leader should always put his or her ego third, behind meeting the mission of the organization first, and the concerns of the people around them second. The PYT concept was easy to understand and

---
[33] Jeffrey Krames, *Inside Drucker's Brain* (New York: The Penguin Group, 2008)

to put into practice, both in their current roles as cadet leaders at the Academy, and after graduation when they would become second lieutenants.

During a graded team project, the cadets expanded on that idea to develop what I now call the Leader's Pyramid. The concept is built and grounded on proven principles and is valuable to all types of leaders, but especially for you as you begin your career. Without experience to draw from, many new managers seem to think they must change their behavior when they become the boss, often becoming "hardnosed" or "tough." That is their definition of how a manager or leader should act. Evidence bears out that being a mean boss is not going to lead to success.

Conversely, a new manager may put too much emphasis on being popular with their subordinates. Leaders should not adopt other people's emotions as their own. In a *Harvard Business Review* article entitled, "What Makes a Leader?" by Daniel Goleman, he writes that it is a mistake to attempt to try to please everybody. Taking the appropriate action under that scenario would be nearly impossible. Instead, Goleman suggests that while considering people's feelings, other factors (such as the mission) is a better way to make intelligent decisions.[34]

Too often, both types of leaders, too tough or too nice, will end up failing because they lack the proper balance in their focus and actions. Legendary UCLA basketball coach John Wooden, whose teams won seven straight NCAA national championships, put the importance of seeking balance this way:

> "Balance is crucial in everything we do. Along with love, it's among the most important things in life. I strove for balance in my leadership and coaching and taught that balance was necessary for Competitive Greatness. The body has to be in balance; the mind has to be in balance; emotions must be in balance. Balance is important in everything we do."[35]

---

34 Daniel Goleman, "What Makes a Leader?", *Harvard Business Review*
35 John Wooden and Steve Jamison, *Wooden on Leadership* (New York:

CLIMB THE LEADER'S PYRAMID (FOR BALANCE AND CONSISTENCY)

Besides proper leadership balance, another goal is that the Leader's Pyramid will provide you a method so that your leadership actions are consistent. People want to be able to go to their boss for a decision or advice and not be worried if the leader is on an emotional roller coaster or out of sorts.

As a new leader, you should be selective in focusing on what is important. In the case of the Leader's Pyramid, those few and important things are mission, people, and ego. The mission refers to what needs to be done to meet organizational objectives. People concerns refer to the needs and desires of the staff or subordinates. Finally, ego refers to a leader's own self-interest. Almost every decision that you make as a leader will factor in one, two, or all three of those elements.

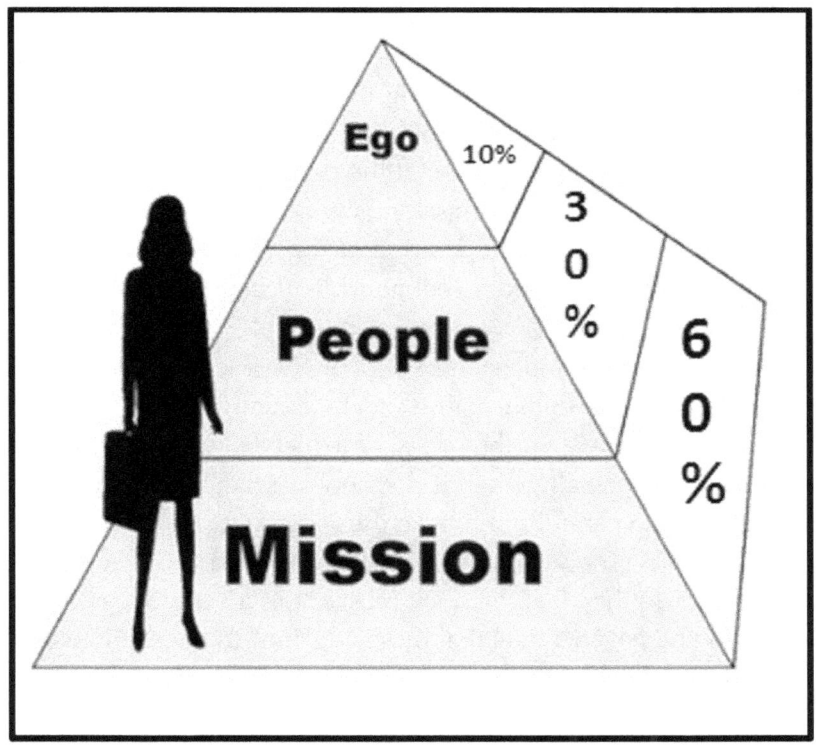

McGraw-Hill, 2005), xv.

Most your time should be squarely on the mission. I believe that 60 percent, the majority, of your time, energy, and focus is necessary on meeting the mission – the most important responsibility of any leader. I suggest that a leader should focus twice as much on mission responsibilities as those of people concerns. That means 30 percent of a leader's time, energy, and focus should be spent on people concerns. Finally, we all have an ego that needs to be part of the leadership equation. Failing to recognize our ego is dangerous and has often been the downfall of many leaders. Therefore, people concerns should be three times that of our own ego, constituting the final 10 percent of the Leader's Pyramid.

Pyramid Base: The Mission

The largest part of the pyramid, the base, symbolizes your organization's mission. As you make your decisions, always keep in mind that you are charged with ensuring that your part achieves its mission. When someone is told, "You look like a person on a mission," it usually is in a positive light – that the person is laser focused to get things done. Performing the mission is why you get a paycheck. You are compensated to run an operation of some kind. You are not paid to always make your workers feel good, and neither are you paid to inflate your own ego.

Your people will understand your role as a leader and decision-maker. They will not hold it against you for making decisions based on the mission first. However, they do want to feel that you are considering their interests, especially when it does not conflict with basic mission requirements. Be careful not to take the mission focus to the extreme. I have seen many new supervisors make a mistake in their decision-making because they feel that they must act in a certain way because they are in charge. They feel that by saying "no" to their followers that they are somehow demonstrating their power and authority.

A 100 percent focus on the mission means that you do not pay enough attention to your people's interests.

CLIMB THE LEADER'S PYRAMID (FOR BALANCE AND CONSISTENCY)

As the base is the most important part of the Leader's Pyramid, the mission is the most important aspect of leadership. A crack in the base of the Leader's Pyramid can lead to a collapse in the overall structure, including your own interests. The pyramid base is the foundation that must be strong enough to support the enormous weight of the Leader's Pyramid. In a similar manner, a leader must also be strong. I refer to the "weight on a leader's shoulders" as the tough decisions that are often necessary. Many of these decisions will involve matters related to the mission, people, and our ego.

Therefore, a leader is well to operate in the most stable and secure part of the pyramid – the base that represents the mission. It is the workplace's primary means for existence in meeting organizational goals. That mission is what a manager ensures gets done.

One manager who clearly understood this idea was legendary Yankee baseball coach Casey Stengel. He introduced several innovative concepts to baseball such as platooning his players to ensure the best individuals played while keeping them fresh for the long season. He even benched one of the best baseball players in history, Joe DiMaggio, and took a future Hall of Fame pitcher Whitey Ford out of a World Series game with only one out to go to ensure the win.

Yogi Berra, who played for Stengel, observed that the coach did not care what anyone thought about his actions as the team leader. Stengel once told a writer, "I'm sorry I had to take the young man (Ford) out, but as I have been telling you, the Philadelphias is hard to defeat, and I am paid by my employer to defeat them, which is why I went for the fella with the big fastball. Have a nice winter."[36]

In a more recent example involving sports, University of Alabama Coach Nick Saban proved why he ranks among the coaching greats. In the 2018 college national football championship game against rival Georgia Bulldogs, the Crimson Tide fell behind 13 to 0 by halftime. In a bold move, Saban replaced his starting quarterback with a freshman who had played very little during the regular season.

---
36 Dave Kaplan and Yogi Berra, *Ten Rings: My Championship Seasons* (New Jersey: William Morrow and Company, 2003)

Asked why he made such an unorthodox move, Saban replied, "I just thought we had to throw the ball in the game, and I thought he could do it better."[37] The result: a thrilling 26 – 23 win over Georgia in overtime and his sixth national title, matching Alabama's own Paul "Bear" Bryant's legendary record. Coach Saban, like Coach Stengel with the Yankees, kept the mission first, even ahead of the feelings of the most visible players on the team.

There was a circumstance where a leader may have put people concerns improperly over mission. The results were disastrous. In the 2003 American League championship, the Boston Red Sox were leading their rival New York Yankees in game seven of the series. Things were looking good for the Bo Sox. They had their pitching ace Pedro Martinez on the mound going into the 8th inning with a three-run lead. The bullpen had performed well during the championship series so if Pedro ran out of gas, they could still finish out the game with a win.

Sure enough, Martinez allowed a hit, then another, and then another as the Yankees cut into the Boston lead. When the Red Sox manager went to the mound to check on his pitcher, Martinez had already exceeded 100 pitches thrown – a number often used as a threshold, especially at the first sign of trouble.

Instead, Martinez convinced the coach that he still had enough to finish the game and secure a victory. Remember, this was the seventh game of the league championship series. There would be no tomorrow for the losing team. The winner, on the other hand, would go on to play in the coveted World Series. Pedro Martinez gave up more hits and more runs until eventually the Red Sox lost the game and the league championship.[38]

Under the Leader's Pyramid structure, the mission and people concerns are not equal. Author Richard Koch called this the "50/50 fallacy." He challenges conventional thinking that there is a natural or almost democratic equilibrium between causes or inputs and results

---

37   "Walk-off: Alabama beats Georgia in OT for national title," by Associated Press, January 09, 2018
38   Ibid.

or outputs.[39] In the case of the Leader's Pyramid, we assign two times the area of the pyramid to the mission (base) compared to the people section (middle tier). Put another way, 60 percent of your decision-making should stem from mission requirements and only 30 percent from people concerns. From that perspective, the decision to override the mission component should be compelling.

In the case of the Boston Red Sox manager, if his team was ahead of the Yankees by a large score (8-0) and they were in the last inning, then maybe the coach would have had more latitude in his decision. In that situation, the mission of winning the league championship does not appear in real jeopardy so he might agree to keep Martinez in with a chance to finish the game and pitch a rare shutout. However, this was not the decision made and the Red Sox organization paid the price. As General Colin Powell once noted, "The mission is what you exist for, and everything is secondary to the mission."[40]

Middle Section: People Focus

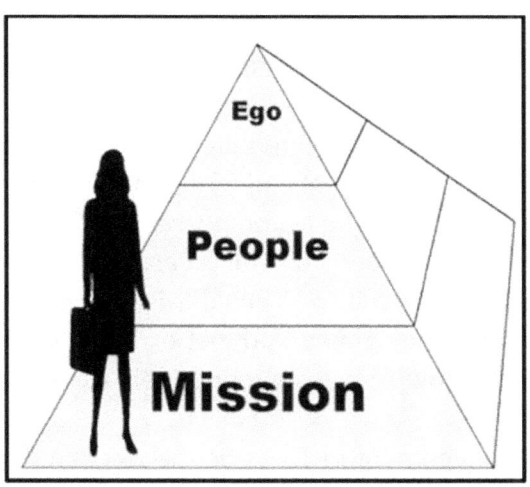

---

39   Richard Koch, *The 80/20 Principle: The Secret to Achieving More with Less* (New York: Doubleday, 2008)
40   Charles Garcia, *Leadership Lessons of the White House Fellow: Learn How to Inspire Others, Achieve Greatness, and Find Success in any Organization* (McGraw-Hill, 2009), 54.

Notice that the people tier, the middle section of the Leader's Pyramid, borders the mission base of the pyramid. It can be difficult sometimes to distinguish where the base (mission) ends and the middle tier (people concerns) begins. When you are in that "border" area, you can only make your best judgement and press on with a decision. Tony Zinni, former General, offers his insights into decision-making involving the middle-tier and people concerns.

> "Choosing good people is not the only people-related decision leaders face. They must also decide what to do when someone isn't measuring up. Offering help (such as counseling or training) is the easy part. It's more difficult to decide whether an individual is salvageable and how hard it will be to salvage them. Can the organization afford the time and effort it would take to bring him around? How will his peers see the investment? Very tough calls."[41]

A 100 percent focus on the people means that you are trying to be best friends, and nothing is done.

Some of you may be thinking that it does not seem right to not put your followers first, even ahead of the mission. After all, without people, the mission cannot be accomplished. As General Powell, and others have rightfully observed, "Take care of the people, and the people will take care of you."[42] While this is true, also remember that when the mission is being met, and met exceptionally well, you are in a better position to take care of your people – the goal of any good leader.

During my assignment in Texas as the Accounting and Finance

---

41 Tony Zinni and Tony Koltz, *Leading the Charge: Leadership Lessons from the Battlefield to the Boardroom* (New York: Palgrave Macmillan), 2009, 197.
42 Charles Garcia, *Leadership Lessons of the White House Fellow: Learn How to Inspire Others, Achieve Greatness, and Find Success in any Organization* (McGraw-Hill, 2009), 112.

Officer of the 100-person organization, we had a stellar reputation. We had won numerous organizational awards and our customer service considered exceptional on the military installation. During a three-year period, our office was recognized twice as the "Best Accounting and Finance Office" in the Air Training Command, the military training headquarters for over a dozen Air Force installations. Everyone in our organization had worked hard to provide top-notch support to the installation mission of training Airmen.

One day, the installation commander, a two-star General Officer, called me that he was on his way to our organization and for me to meet him in the customer lobby. When he arrived, he raised his arms and brought the surprised audience of customers and office workers to silence. The popular General then proceeded to call one of our Sergeants (non-commissioned officer) to the front of the lobby. Dave, a Technical Sergeant (E-6) made the short walk from where he was standing in the back and saluted smartly the General.

The Commander's aide then handed to the General a set of new stripes. You see, the General was exercising new authority granted to commanders to selectively and immediately promote an enlisted person under the STEP program – Stripes To Exceptional Performers. The General commended Dave for all his outstanding work and pinned the new stripes on him. At that moment, a shocked and speechless Technical Sergeant Dave became Master Sergeant Dave (E-7)! A lobby full of customers, and Dave's proud staff and teammates, all erupted with heartfelt cheers.

I take nothing away from Dave's accomplishments that led to that promotion. I was the one who nominated him for the STEP promotion in the first place. However, I am convinced that it was in many ways due to the outstanding reputation of the entire Accounting and Finance Office – 100 strong – that also worked in Dave's favor and led him to his big moment. The General, in promoting Dave, was also rewarding the good work of the entire Accounting and Finance organization. Mission success can lead to similar victories for your people.

People Focus: Importance of Motivation and Ability

As a new leader, be careful not to look at your organization's performance as if reading the daily newspaper to review your stock investment performance. Sometimes it might be up (a good thing), but sometimes it is down (a bad thing). You just hope the next day is better.

Years ago, I created a successful formula, a roadmap that has framed how I try to treat people. It is called the MAP formula.

$$\text{Motivation} \times \text{Ability} = \text{Performance}$$

By concentrating on the right side of the equation (performance), a leader is merely looking at performance in a snapshot in time. The MAP formula suggests that a leader instead concentrate on the left side of the equation, motivation and ability. These factors determine performance and can be directly influenced by a leader.

Let us look at two scenarios involving two new leaders, Jane and John. In scenario one, Jane's followers were very motivated. She treats them with respect and dignity, seeks to know them on a personal level, and encourages their ideas and rewards them for their efforts. For discussion sake, let's quantify her people's motivation at the highest possible percentage, 100 percent.

However, Jane did fail in ensuring that her staff had the proper resources to do the job. Their computer equipment was not up to date and frequently crashed causing work delays. She did not properly submit her budget request on time that led to inadequate training and professional development opportunities. The office environment was less than ideal. Thus, we quantify their ability at 70 percent, a lower percentage than the motivation factor. If you multiplied their motivation level (100 percent) times their ability level (70 percent), performance would be 70 percent.

In the second scenario, John always stayed in his office, never associating much with his team. He instead concentrated on the right manager duties such as ensuring his people had the proper resources, training, etc., to be ABLE to perform well. Let us quantify his staff's ability at a high 100 percent.

However, in this case, John did not "rally the troops" in the manner that Jane had done. Because John always stayed in his office, sometimes with the door closed, he never connected with his people. Frankly, John did not care about their personal lives or what made them tick. John felt that they were paid a salary and that is all the reward they should be entitled. John's staff were unmotivated. We are generous with a motivation level of 60 percent. If we multiplied motivation (60 percent) times their ability level (100 percent), their performance level would equal 60 percent.

You see, a leader needs to do both things. Provide motivation and ensure that ability is also high. Doing one well, and the other poor, will always result in a less than optimal performance. Remember, M X A = P.

Let us illustrate the importance of maximizing both components that lead to performance. Take a simple grading scale that you may have seen in your college courses.

$$90 \text{ to } 100 \text{ percent} = A$$
$$80 \text{ to } 89 \text{ percent} = B$$
$$70 \text{ to } 79 \text{ percent} = C$$
$$60 \text{ to } 69 \text{ percent} = D$$

Notice that the MAP formula is a multiplicative equation, not addition or subtraction. If your employees have a <u>90 percent motivation level</u>, that would be considered an "A" on our simple grading scale. If they have a <u>90 percent ability level</u>, that would also be an "A" on our scoring. You would assume that an "A" times an "A" would mean an "A" in performance, right?

That is not the case. If your staff is not *fully* motivated (in this case, 90 percent means that they are 10 percent short), nor do they have the *maximum* ability (also 10 percent short), when you multiply 90 percent motivation times 90 percent ability that would only be

81 percent performance. Instead of an "A" performance level, they would only be at a "B" grade instead.

Only when you have a group that is completely motivated and completely able, are you not leaving any performance potential behind. Therefore, strive for 100 percent motivation *and* ability to attain the maximum performance.

The Apex: Managing your Ego

"Leaders who focus on external gratification instead of inner satisfaction find it difficult to stay grounded."[43]

From the book, True North *by Bill George and Peter Sims*

Look once more at the Leader's Pyramid below. Notice that the ego section of the pyramid is the farthest away from the base of the pyramid where a leader's focus is on the mission. The leader can experience what even expert mountain climbers face – altitude sickness. Thus, you are not firmly grounded and at your best point as a leader.

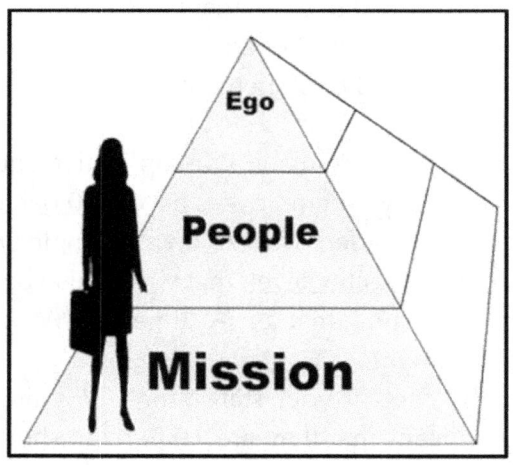

---

43   Bill George and Peter Sims, *True North: Discover your Authentic Leadership* (San Francisco: Jossey-Bass, 2007), 29.

When leaders find themselves at its very apex, the highest ten percent of the Leader's Pyramid, they can begin to feel light-headed. They can feel giddy because their self-esteem is being stroked, or because they have nice surroundings. As is the case with real climbing, you are in danger when you stay at such altitude for a long period. The best thing to do is climb down from the apex back to the firm footing found at the most secure part of the pyramid, the base.

As a new graduate, recognize that humility is not weakness for a leader. In their book, *Egonomics*, David Marcum and Steven Smith note that humility is a positive trait. The authors list humility, along with curiosity and veracity as the three principles of Egonomics that keep ego working as an asset rather than as a liability. They make the case that humility is intelligent self-respect that keeps us from thinking too much or too little of ourselves. It reminds us how far we have come while at the same time helping us see how far short we are of what can be.[44] People associate humility with weakness or being timid and not strength. Humility includes confidence, ambition, and willpower.[45]

Therefore, we see that ego is not a bad thing. Ego, or a variant of ego such as pride, can compel you to do well at work and in your personal life. There is nothing wrong with trying to feel good or to gain some stature among family, friends, and associates.

My concern occurs when a leader makes decisions by first regarding how she or he will look from those decisions. You can share pride with others, but you cannot share ego if it is a selfish emotion.

100 percent focus on ego builds a house of cards. It looks good for the moment but is ready to fall anytime.

The importance of ego management is significant enough for a new college graduate that we devote the next chapter to that principle.

---

[44] David Marcum and Steven Smith, *Egonomics: What makes ego our greatest asset (or most expensive liability)* (New York: Simon and Schuster, 2008), 27.
[45] Ibid.

How to use the Leader's Pyramid

We built the pyramid one section at a time. We started with the pyramid base that represents the most important element of leadership – getting the mission accomplished. Then, we added the middle tier, which represents people concerns. Finally, at the very top, we added the apex that represents our own ego, or self-interest. Now that we have built it, we can use the Leader's Pyramid as a valuable tool and a practical means to stay focused on the mission, people, and our own ego.

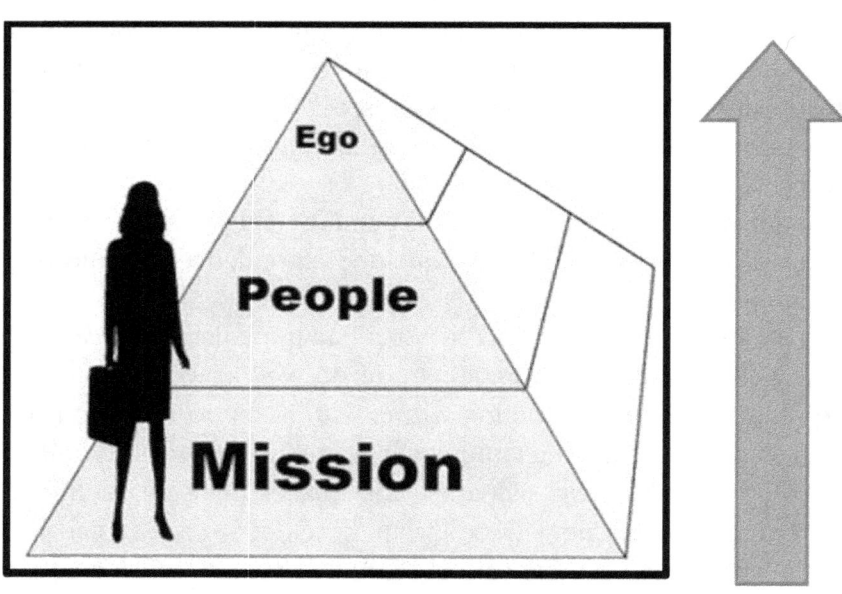

Starting at the bottom of the Leader's Pyramid may seem a little unnatural to use in our "top down" way of thinking. Starting at the bottom of the pyramid keeps us grounded in our decision-making. If your decision affects the mission, then decide accordingly. Whenever possible, you should strive to reach the next level, people concerns, if the mission is not negatively impacted. Sometimes you have no other choice but to stay in the base, the mission component.

The Mission comes First

As an Air Force squadron commander, I faced daily challenges associated with meeting our important mission. A young troop, let us call her "Mindy" was up for reenlistment (a contract for another four years). As her commander, it was up to me to make a final decision to allow her to reenlist or to deny it, forcing her separation from military service.

In Mindy's case, it was not a routine or easy decision. Although she was a solid performer, she had received two non-judicial punishments in her first term of enlistment. This was very unusual. A non-judicial punishment is a way of dealing with poor behavior without a full-blown court-martial proceeding. Her last punishment occurred only a few months earlier where she was in a deployment area while she served in support of the global war on terrorism operations.

There is a formal process for reenlistment in the Air Force. It was not just my own judgment as her commander, but that of her immediate supervisor and others in her chain-of-command that factored into the decision. Repeatedly, her supervisors backed Mindy's request to reenlist, citing her pleasant demeanor and work ethic. Again, I had no problem with that part of the equation and if nothing else were in play, I would have gladly signed the paperwork and offered to conduct the reenlistment ceremony myself.

I did have a problem, however, with her receiving two separate non-judicial punishments, especially the one involving the overseas deployment. Our ability to function in wartime or a military exercise separates us from our civilian counterparts.

I decided that because the mission of the military, the Air Force, and my squadron, it was not in the best interest to allow Mindy to reenlist. As much as I too liked her personally, it would not be fair to those who had met the required standards. If I allowed her to reenlist, what kind of signal would that send to her peers?

My decision was not a popular one. This is where a tool or principle like the Leader's Pyramid can assist you as you start your career and face these types of tough decisions. Do you lean towards people concerns? Alternatively, do you defer to the mission instead? The right answer is to think mission *first*. I do not know many people fired for meeting the mission.

I felt vindicated when my own boss, the installation commander (General Officer) supported my decision when it was appealed to him. I had started in the base of the Leader's Pyramid, representing mission concerns, and I could not justify why I should move from the grounded and firm footing to the next higher tier.

To finish, there is a positive side to this story. Years later, Brenda and I ran into Mindy and her family in a completely different city. By that time, I had retired from the Air Force to begin my second career as a civilian. When she saw me, Mindy genuinely hugged me and told us how happy she was as a college student and that she had a clearer focus on her life after separating from military service. I felt even better about my decision because it seemed that all parties came out ahead.

When the Mission is met, People concerns can be addressed

Former Tennessee Titans head coach Jeff Fisher could move from the bottom of the pyramid (mission) to the next level, people concerns. Coach Fisher had the most regular season National Football League wins over a five-year period. His image is one of a "no ego" nice person who can still be tough when necessary. He believes in meeting his people's needs, especially if achieving the mission of winning football games. He once said, "The one thing that I always keep in mind is how the players are feeling and whether they are tired or not or whether they're sore. You have to adjust, and you have to do things for them."[46]

Coach Fisher was the first NFL coach to allow players to live at home while attending the training camp. If the mission of training camp is achieved, including the proper physical training, coming together as a team, and executing the playbook, then there was no

---

46 Tom Weir, "Don't Mess with nice guy Fisher," *USA Today*, January 2, 2004

real reason why the players could not live at home while attending training camp. The coach added, "You have to have an environment where people want to come to work."[47]

A second chance to reach People concerns tier

Unlike the case with Mindy, who I denied reenlistment opportunity, there was another case where I could accommodate people concerns while achieving our mission requirements. As mentioned earlier, during one of my military assignments, our installation faced an Operational Readiness Inspection (ORI). Occurring every few years, the ORI is an important measurement of how the squadrons and the base are performing its mission. Getting ready for an ORI visit can take up to six months to properly plan and execute.

As my own squadron was nearing final preparation, I discovered an excellent job opportunity for one of my officers named Dwayne. He had done an excellent job as a Financial Services Officer and the new position at the higher headquarters level would lead to increased responsibility and improved promotion potential. The problem was that the gaining unit wanted Dwayne to be reassigned immediately, a month or so before the inspection.

Saying no to the other unit would have been perfectly reasonable on my part. After all, there was a direct impact on our mission performance since Dwayne played a key role in my squadron and in our preparation for the inspection. Furthermore, our unit and individual careers are made or broken on the outcome of the demanding two-week inspection, including my own.

Yet, I knew Dwayne deserved better. Rather, than deciding based on the mission alone, certainly understandable, I sought a compromise with the gaining unit to let us hold on to Dwayne until our ORI was completed. I told the other commander that if they could wait until the day after the inspection, we had a deal.

Thus, I achieved a "win-win" outcome. The mission was accomplished, as evidenced by our great inspection rating, one of the best

---

47 Ibid.

in our squadron's history. That is the first win. Secondly, a happy officer (Dwayne) went on to an improved opportunity. In fact, moving Dwayne who was a Captain at the time meant that one of our young Lieutenants could backfill Dwayne and thus promoted in his job responsibilities. Win number two: people desires and needs were also met. If you factor in that the inspection was something to be proud of, along with building a reputation for taking care of people, my own ego was stroked. That means a rare, "win-win-win" situation – thanks to the Leader's Pyramid principle.

Summary: Benefit of the Leader's Pyramid

Repeatedly, I used and continue to use the Leader's Pyramid principle to make similar tough calls. I do not suggest that the tool is completely infallible. However, I am suggesting that the principle is a good starting point in your decision-making.

As a new graduate, the Leader's Pyramid can provide you a frame of reference that you can use on a day-to-day basis to help you make optimal decisions. The structure is important because you now have a balanced framework about a few things – the mission, people, and ego – and the right mix among the elements (60/30/10 percent respectively).

Your actions will also be more consistent. As you make decisions, follow the basic approach outlined. Start at the bottom and work your way up the pyramid. Do so even when, and especially, if there are pressures on you to make a quick decision. Use the Leader's Pyramid each time, and your decisions will be consistent, and I believe often the right one.

CHAPTER 5

Manage your ego (as one manages cholesterol)

HAVING EGO IS like having cholesterol. There are two types that flow through our veins. The good cholesterol, high-density lipoprotein or HDL seems to carry cholesterol away from the arteries and back to the liver where it can be passed from the body, thus reducing the risk of heart disease. Conversely, too much low-density lipoprotein or LDL is not a good thing because this form of bad cholesterol can build up slowly in the inner walls of the arteries that feed the heart and brain, potentially forming plaque that narrows the arteries. This can lead to clot that blocks a narrowed artery and a heart attack or stroke can be the result.[48]

Similarly, to managing our cholesterol, we must manage our ego. Some form of ego may be useful and good for us. However, bad ego can be harmful to us if not kept in check.

In his work, *The Little Book on Big Ego*, Joel Epstein makes the case that if a leader's ego is healthy (good), they tend to empower others around them and that leads to more energy in the organization. Epstein calls the effect Positive Friction. He concludes, "Ego is a wonderful thing. A healthy ego results in productive self-confidence. With self-confidence, different options can be considered, and correct

---
48 American Heart Association, website: http://www.americanheart.org

decisions made. Success is realized, goals are met."⁴⁹

On the other hand, I have seen too many leaders who take out more energy out of the organization then they put into it. The primary reason is due to an unhealthy or bad ego. Epstein refers to the situation where a boss feels compelled to run everything themselves as Negative Friction. Pathetically, a boss may refuse to empower others because of the fear that someone other than them will look good.[50]

Good Ego

> "I confess that I desire to be re-elected. I have the common pride of humanity to wish my past four years administration endorsed; and besides I honestly believe that I can better serve the nation in its need and peril than any new man could possibly do."[51]
>
> *President Abraham Lincoln*

In an article entitled "Level 5 Leadership: The Triumph of Humility and Fierce Resolve," Jim Collins describes a great leader as one who sits at the highest of his five hierarchies or levels. A rare level 5 leader is someone who leaves an enduring legacy for greatness. The author makes the case that truly transformative leaders possess a paradoxical mix of humility and will. While timid, they are also ferocious. Shy yet fearless. Collins describes President Lincoln as a Level 5 leader who "never let his ego get in the way of his ambitions to create an enduring great nation."[52]

There will be times when your own self-worth can be fed in a

---

49 Joel Epstein, *The Little Book on Big Ego: A Guide to Manage and Control the EGOMANICAS in Your Life* (Rockville: Alnola Productions, 2006), 110.
50 Ibid, 77-78.
51 Doris Kearns Goodwin, *Team of Rivals: The Political Genius of Abraham Lincoln* (New York: Simon and Schuster, 2005), 648.
52 Jim Collins, "Level 5 Leadership: The Triumph of Humility and Fierce Resolve," *Harvard Business Review*, 2001

variety of ways. Being part of upper management, having a nice office, perhaps your own assistant, and many other "perks" that your company might offer. Chris Brady and Orrin Woodward wrote in their book, *Launching a Leadership Revolution*, "There are definitely perks and privileges that come with successful leadership, and they are enjoyable and flattering. But these rewards are not the purpose of leadership, they are merely the side benefits."[53]

Another consideration is that your own people's hard work leads to your own success. Do not get consumed by your own ego at your follower's expense, or even worse, at the expense of your organization. If that happens, frankly, you are no good to anybody.

Bad Ego

"Politics gives guys so much power and such big egos they tend to behave badly toward women. And I hope I never get into that."

William Jefferson Clinton

Renowned leadership author John Maxwell had this to say about excessive pride or ego. "A prideful person will have a tendency to look down on other people, feeling a sense of superiority. People will not follow or identify with a snobbish personality who is conscious of status or position."[54]

In their book, *Power Ambition Glory: The Stunning Parallels between Great Leaders of the Ancient World and Today...and the Lessons You Can Learn*, Steve Forbes and John Prevas note that "the real challenge of leadership, as we saw with Alexander and Caesar, is to maintain character in the face of success. Leadership brings with it a host of temptations, opportunities, for enormous personal gain,

---

53 Chris Brady and Orrin Woodward, *Launching a Leadership Revolution: Mastering the Five Levels of Influence* (New York: Business Plus, 2005), 216.
54 John Maxwell, *Be a People Person: Effective Leadership through Effective Relationships* (Colorado Springs: David Cook, 2007), 41.

adulation, and inflated egos, all of which can become a toxic brew"[55]

Apparently, ego challenges have been around a long time.

Ego Management

According to the Mayo Clinic, there are numerous ways to manage cholesterol levels to minimize the negative effect. Examples include:[56]

    A. Eating heart-healthy foods
    B. Exercise regularly
    C. Do not or quit smoking
    D. Lose weight
    E. Drink alcohol in moderation

In the same manner as there are ways to managing bad cholesterol, we can seek means to manage our good and bad ego.

As we have repeatedly stated, ego is not detrimental if kept in check. A leader with confidence and pride is more apt to make the hard calls and necessary decisions in the toughest of times. However, it can be a slippery slope when a leader's pride can turn to overconfidence and make poor decisions as a result.

As a new leader, how then do you assess if you are on that slippery slope regarding your own ego? In his book *Ego Check: Why Executive Hubris is Wrecking Companies and Careers and How to Avoid the Trap*, Mathew Hayward analyzes various business leaders who have crashed and burned because of their arrogance and reckless ways. Hayward acknowledges that while pride is a vital and important emotion in the workplace to possess, an ego check framework allows grounded decision-making. Essentially, he encourages leaders to (1) not make decisions with undue pride, (2) delegate properly and let

---

55 Steve Forbes and Jean Prevas, *Power Ambition Glory: The Stunning Parallels between Great Leaders of the Ancient World and Today...and the Lessons You can Learn* (New York: Crown Business, 2009), 284.
56 Mayo Clinic website, found at https://www.mayoclinic.org/diseases-conditions/high-blood-cholesterol/in-depth/reduce-cholesterol/art-20045935

the right people decide certain things, (3) seize the feedback of others, and (4) see through the consequences of your decisions.⁵⁷

A Final Caution

As a new college graduate, you should certainly be proud of your accomplishments. I still remember the day I graduated from the University of Arizona in Tucson, Arizona. My path was a bit different from a traditional student, as I had spent eight years as an enlisted person in the United States Air Force. While attending the U of A full-time, I worked a part-time job to make ends meet for my family. My last semester was especially difficult as my mother became sick and passed away during that time. Frankly, I was not sure I would make it across the finish line, but I did. Going through that kind of adversity gave me the confidence to tackle challenges that would come later in my career and life.

As you begin your career, always be willing to be open-minded enough to value the opinion of others, especially those with more experience then you have right now. Former Speaker of the House Tip O'Neill once told a story worth sharing. A colleague in the House of Representatives told O'Neill about someone who seemed to have a good track record of predicting which group of new congressmen would be successful or not. Instead of a powerful Committee Chairman or political boss, the wise person turned out to be a doorkeeper. After one election, the future Speaker went up to the doorkeeper and asked him his opinion of the new crop of freshmen Congressmen. His response was, "Well, there are four fellows out there that won't be coming back." When asked why he thought so, the doorkeeper replied:⁵⁸

> "They're just down here and still wet behind the ears. They do not know what it is all about, but by God, they think they are

---

57 Matthew Hayward, *Ego Check: Why Executive Hubris is Wrecking Companies and Careers and How to Avoid the Trap* (Chicago: Kaplan Publishing, 2007)
58 Thomas "Tip" O'Neill and William Novak, *Man of the House: The Life and Political Memories of Speaker Tip O'Neill* (New York: Random House, 1987), 196.

the experts on everything. Now the way I figure it, if they act this way in front of their fellow members who are the real experts, imagine what they must be like back home. They must be insufferable! Just about every time I see a young man come in here who thinks he knows more than his colleagues, he gets licked."[59]

In summary, be confident in your abilities but not overconfident. Learn from others. As we stated in a previous chapter, the principle of effective listening will go a long way as you embark on your career journey. As Robert Schuller succinctly captured it, "Big egos have little ears."[60]

---

59 Ibid.
60 Found at website https://www.azquotes.com/quote/1308654

CHAPTER **6**

Diversity: A complete leader leads all people

> "I never felt I could be a complete professional without having won the British Open. It was something you had to do to complete your career."
>
> *Arnold Palmer, legendary golf professional*

WE OFTEN SEE or hear the term *complete or total* when referring to someone who has mastered an art or skill. A complete pitcher depicts in my mind someone who has a wide repertoire of pitches (curve ball, fast ball, slider pitch, etc.) and has the stamina to go well into the late innings of a game. A total piano player has a reputation for excellence in rhythm, pace, and a good ear for the accompanying music

You cannot consider yourself a complete leader, a total leader, if you are not leading all your people. If somebody's talent is left behind, you are not maximizing your organization's performance. You must lead everyone in your department, not just the ones you like. If any person is not participating, then they are not contributing. If someone is not contributing fully, you are going to come up short in meeting your mission. Your organizational performance will be less than 100 percent. This is the value of promoting diversity. The individuals have a chance to reach their highest potential and the organization's performance is advanced. A win-win situation.

In her book, *Team of Rivals: The Political Genius of Abraham Lincoln*, author Doris Kearns Goodwin describes a situation involving Lincoln's cabinet member Samuel Chase. A former Governor of Ohio, and later Treasury Secretary, Chase continuously sought to undermine Lincoln to seek his own ambition to become President. In fact, Lincoln had even fired Chase once because he was such a disruptive force in his cabinet. Despite these feelings, Lincoln appointed him as Chief Justice of the Supreme Court, a position Chase coveted.[61]

Chase's friend John Alley of Massachusetts praised Lincoln: "Mr. President, this is an exhibition of magnanimity and patriotism that could hardly be expected of any one. After what he (Chase) has said against your administration, which has undoubtedly been reported to you, it was hardly to be expected that you would bestow the most important office within your gift on such a man."[62]

Lincoln later admitted that he would rather have swallowed a buckhorn chair than to have nominated Chase. Yet, Lincoln did not allow ego to get in the way of this important decision. He said, "To have done otherwise I should have been recreant to my convictions of duty to the Republican party and to the country."[63]

President Lincoln put his mission as Chief Executive of the nation ahead of his own personal likes and dislikes. In doing so, Lincoln gives us a valuable lesson to emulate. I have not always personally liked all my bosses, my peers, and my followers. Like most of you, I have my "buttons" that can be pushed and sometimes they are deliberately pushed. However, to be a complete leader, you must lead all your people with the same enthusiasm and energy. It takes a superior leader to not make an adverse decision based on ruffled feathers but

---

61 Doris Kearns Goodwin, *Team of Rivals: The Political Genius of Abraham Lincoln* (New York: Simon and Schuster, 2005), 679.
62 Ibid, 680.
63 Ibid.

instead always stay focused on the mission at hand.

Similarly, a complete leader must accept differences within the group and not be bothered by them. I was serving overseas when President Clinton instituted the "don't ask, don't tell" policy. One of my troops asked me in passing what I thought about the change. Without hesitation, I said if a person is part of the team and contributes to the mission that is all that matters to me. She almost seemed disappointed with my quick answer, and even teased me a bit about it, but I was not going there.

If a leader excludes anyone from participating, and contributing, for whatever reason, the mission will suffer. Look at the impact of President Lincoln's decision to allow black soldiers into the Civil War fight. He noted in August 1864, "Take from us and give to the enemy the hundred and thirty, forty, or fifty thousand colored persons now serving us as soldiers, seamen, and laborers and we cannot longer maintain the contest."[64]

The same concept applies, especially today, to people of different race, creed, religion, age, gender, orientation, or something not so obvious. If any person or group are held back and have a glass ceiling imposed on them, then you also have a glass ceiling on your ability to meet your own mission objectives.

My proudest individual award is recognition as the Male Boss of the Year through the Federal Woman's Program at a major military installation. The award was special because it was the women in my organization who got together to nominate me for the award, not my boss. I had encouraged them to succeed in their own endeavors, but also ensuring that we had everyone participating and contributing to our organizational success.

I must admit though, during my 28-year years of military service, there was a time when I had an arrogant attitude about those who served as "weekend" warriors in the guard or reserve. That began to change when I was assigned to the Pentagon in Washington, DC

---

64 The Lincoln Institute Presents, Mr. Lincoln and Freedom, website: http://www.mrlincolnandfreedom.org

working in the Office of Air Force Reserve. I was in the building when it was attacked on September 11, 2001.

9-11 Changes my Perspective

On that fateful morning, I was proceeding to our command section on the other side of the Pentagon, where I ran into my boss. He asked me if I heard what had just occurred in New York City and I told him that I had not. We stepped into the nearby Public Affairs office that had a television set on and started watching the horrific news unfold. After what seemed only a few minutes, we heard and slightly felt a thud directly on the opposite side of the Pentagon – one of the world's largest office buildings. It was 9.38 a.m. Eastern Standard Time.

We turned to our left, and since we were on the fifth floor (highest) and there were windows, we saw flames and black smoke directly across from us. Someone, logically perhaps but incorrectly, shouted that a bomb had gone off on the rooftop. In reality, it was the crash of Flight number 77. We were witnessing the momentum of the flames and smoke going over the roof from the opposite side of the crash site.

Without any panic, those of us in the room joined others who started walking down the hall toward the nearest exit. What has always amazed me was that in a matter of only minutes, there were people in place directing us to the right stairways to exit the building. When I had made it outside, I ran into an Army Lieutenant Colonel friend of mine and we went to see what had happened. As we approached the smoke and flames, someone directed us to assist with controlling a perimeter they had just set up. Along with a few others, we were told just to keep people away from disturbing the triage site and allow emergency vehicles to get through without a crowd to navigate. Trust me, my friend and I did absolutely nothing special. There were, however, some incredible acts of bravery occurring nearby as first responders and personnel assigned to the Pentagon began assisting others.

Only then did we realize that this was a third terrorist attack. I was directly in front of the crash site -- watching a wedge in the building that represents our nation's military strength – burn in flames. My eyes were seeing it happen, but my brain had a hard time processing the scene.

After a short while, the police started shouting urgently at us to move away from the Pentagon building, including my Army friend and me. We were pushed back all the way to Interstate 395, a major thoroughfare. It was not the crumbling wedge that was the concern. Word was out that another hijacked plane was returning to Washington, D.C. and that the Pentagon might be under a second attack (as had the New York City Twin Towers).

As I was looking back at the burning Pentagon, standing alongside the I-395 guardrail, there suddenly appeared a single F-16 fighter jet screaming overhead. The F-16 is one of the premier fighter aircrafts in the United States Air Force inventory. When I first saw the awesome plane, I thought to myself, "All right the good guys have arrived! Now we are safe."

Then I caught myself and asked, "Safe from what?" This was not the traditional combat air patrol (CAP) mission that our fighter jets flew when I was deployed to Saudi Arabia, participating in Operation Southern Watch. Back then, our pilots enforced the no-fly zone over southern Iraq to ensure Saddam Hussein could not pose harm on the Shiite population. Any aircraft that dared go up in the no-fly zone faced a fully armed aircraft ready to destroy it. However, in this case, there was no enemy aircraft – only a commercial plane that had been turned into a terrorist weapon.

Of course, that plane never made it back to Washington, D.C. Passengers like Todd Beamer and other heroes decided to take down Flight 93 shortly after 10 a.m., rather than allowing the terrorists another lucrative target.

After the 9-11 attacks, I had an increased exposure to the many reservists and guardsmen called to fight and defend our country. I gained a newfound and tremendous respect for their commitment, dedication, and performance. From that standpoint, they were no different from their active duty counterparts. In fact, they offer a tremendous value to our nation's taxpayers. The Air Force reservists for example, use about six percent of the total budget but fly approximately 25 percent of the military flying missions. That is a great return-on-investment.

The first pilots to reach New York City and the Pentagon shortly after the attacks were Guardsmen: Lt Col Tim Duffy of the 102nd Fighter Wing, Massachusetts National Guard, flying an F-15 fighter aircraft, and Major Dean Eckmann of the 119th Fighter Wing, North Dakota National Guard, flying an F-16 fighter jet.

Imagine not using the guard or reserve forces because we thought they were different somehow or not up to the task. The same holds true today for all our brave reservists and guardsmen in all military branches who have taken the fight to our enemies, serving multiple deployments in tough combat conditions. Fortunately, we have gained a greater appreciation of their contributions to our national defense as part of the total force.

The experience during 9-11 reinforced my belief that a team cannot be a total or complete team if you do not allow everyone in it. Moreover, you cannot be a total or complete leader, unless you are leading the entire team.

The Value of Diversity

I give great credit to Mr. Gil Jamieson, the person in charge of the FEMA Hurricane Katrina recovery efforts, headquartered in New Orleans, for promoting diversity and inclusion. Shortly after reporting in to the recovery office, I volunteered to be a speaker for Hispanic Heritage Month. We formed a small committee of volunteers and put together a nice event for the New Orleans-based workforce. Keep in mind, for most disasters that FEMA provides support to state and local governments, the emphasis tends to be more short-term in nature. Who has time to worry about a special observance month activity? With Hurricane Katrina recovery, we were going to be there for the long-term, five years and beyond. In my mind, this meant that the practices encouraged for most federal agencies applied to us as well. As the Katrina CFO, I encouraged these events as part of doing the recovery business. Most employees worked long hours in austere conditions. We needed to get along to be productive. I set a very conservative budget of between $500 to $1,000 for special observances at each of the recovery offices in the Gulf Coast – a real bargain and a positive return-on-investment as far as I was concerned.

When Gil heard of what we had done for Hispanic Heritage Month in the New Orleans office, he sent me to speak to all the recovery offices. I drove to our locations in Biloxi, Montgomery, Baton Rouge, and the only venue I took a commercial flight, Texas. Mr. Jamieson encouraged all the state directors to get behind the initiative and they certainly did so with gusto.

We continued to build on this initial momentum and continued with other observances including for African-American Heritage Month a few months later. I invited my good friend L.C. Williams to speak to us in New Orleans and he even did so at his own expense, refusing to take federal funding for his travel expenses. L.C. is a great speaker and gave a rousing speech that inspired people in attendance. Promoting the value of diversity in the workplace through special observance months is one way a new leader can get involved.

Diversity and Problem Solving

In this chapter, we have emphasized that to be a complete leader, you must involve and lead all the people in your organization, not a select few. If anybody is left behind, then you've also left behind someone who can contribute, their different viewpoints and ideas. In our next chapter, we will use the principle of a complete leader using diversity and inclusion, to supplement another key principle, Using Creativity to Solve Problems. I must admit, it is perhaps my favorite chapter in the book and one of the most valuable to a new graduate. In one of the studies cited in the introduction chapter, the 2016 Workforce-Skills Preparedness Report, the number one soft skill that hiring managers felt new grads was lacking was critical thinking and problem solving – a whopping 60 percent of managers agreed on this missing trait.[65] Leveraging diversity of others helps, but as you will see, it starts with you and a positive outlook.

---

65 "Leveling Up: How to Win In the Skills Economy," the 2016 Workforce-Skills Preparedness Report

CHAPTER 7

Using creativity to solve problems

"Creativity can solve almost any problem."

George Lois, American art director

YOUR NEW COLLEGE degree, as it did for me, will sooner or later elevate you into the management ranks. Along with the benefits, come the challenges of leadership, including the burden of solving problems. This seventh principle, using creativity to solve problems, addresses the number one soft skill that hiring managers identified as lacking in recent college graduates per the Workforce-Skills Preparedness Report.

In this chapter, we discuss ways to improve on this important attribute, that as a leader, you will face daily. The first step, as you will read, begins with a positive mind.

Optimism makes a difference

In the book, *The Inspiring Leader: Unlocking The Secrets of How Extraordinary Leaders Motivate*, the authors make the case that the research confirms that people who are more optimistic, enjoy greater success in their careers and in their personal lives, and contribute more to their communities. One national insurance company learned that agents that scored higher on an optimism instrument, outsold their pessimistic peers by as high as 57 percent.[66]

A Positive Mind leads to Creativity

"Creativity is a natural extension of our enthusiasm."

Earl Nightingale, American author

The phrases that admittedly make me cringe are ones like, "We've tried that before...", "We can't do that," or "That will never work." The reason is that negativity, the opposite of being positive, shuts down options that you want and need to effectively solve a problem.

There are several reasons why those around you may respond negatively. Most common is that your new ideas may come across as challenging what has been tried before. As a friend once told me, always be tactful in "honoring the past."

The key is to rise above the negativity and remain positive. You can control your own attitude. As Robert Schuller once observed, "Problems are not stop signs, they are guidelines."

The first step then is to frame the encountered problem with the right attitude. In his article, "Winston Churchill makes a fine movie star. If only we had a leader to match him in real life today," Andrew Rawnsley references the new movie release *Darkest Hour*, a story about the former British Prime Minister's framing of the Nazi early dominance over other European countries that was on the doorsteps of England itself.[67] In short order, Hitler had swallowed up Austria, Czechoslovakia, Denmark, Norway, Belgium, Holland, and most striking, his army marched into Paris on June 14, 1940.

Just weeks into his new role as Prime Minster, instead of accepting

---

66 Jack Zenger, Joe Folkman, and Scott Edinger, *The Inspiring Leader: Unlocking the Secrets of How Extraordinary Leaders Motivate* (New York: McGraw-Hill Education, 2009), 37.
67 "Winston Churchill makes a fine movie star. If only we had a leader to match him in real life today," The Observer, January 2018

an offer for a brokered peace with Germany's Adolf Hitler, Churchill rallied and eventually convinced the nation to take on the Nazis and fight for freedom.[68] I often quote Churchill's belief that, "A pessimist sees the difficulty in every opportunity; an optimist sees the opportunity in every difficulty." My natural optimism has served me well.

The United States had its own optimistic leader in President Ronald Reagan. He elegantly spoke of American optimism when he said, "We Americans have never been pessimists. We conquer fear with faith, and we overwhelm threats and hardship with courage, work, opportunity, and freedom."[69]

Whereas Churchill faced the direct threat of Hitler's marching army, Reagan confronted the Soviet Union during the cold war. History will forever remember both men's positive nature in leading both of their countries to victory.

Personality type and Creativity

Some of you may be thinking that you may not be naturally creative because you tend to not be a charismatic leader like Churchill or Reagan who is out front and eloquent in speech. A recent study shows the opposite may be true.

In a *Washington Post* article entitled, "People who seek solitude are more creative, study finds," SUNY Buffalo is credited with a revelation that there is a linkage between certain social withdrawal and increased creativity.[70]

Psychologists studied college students who were not necessarily shy, avoiding interaction with others, but rather, those that were comfortable enough to seek out and enjoy solitude. They were being unsociable, a term used to describe students who deliberately sought out solitude. This group scored higher on creativity.[71]

---

68   Ibid.
69   Found at website https://reaganquotes.wordpress.com/2009/06/13/we-overwhelm-threats-with-freedom/
70   *The Washington Post*, "People who seek solitude are more creative, study finds," Christopher Ingraham, November 22, 2017
71   Ibid.

Other research supports the SUNY Buffalo study. One report explored how solitude may have an association with creativity, and other traits like freedom, intimacy, and spirituality. If you spend time alone, you are less prone to impression management, that can impose a certain pattern of behavior to fit in. This addresses a barrier discussed later regarding sticking with established patterns.

For those of you that are sometimes ridiculed for wanting to spend time alone, realize that isolation may be allowing you time to think, reflect, and seek creativity that could be used to solve problems.

Creativity leads to Prosperity

The Global Creativity Index or GCI is a measure that ranks 139 nations for economic growth and sustainable prosperity. The research correlates economic prosperity to creativity. The three dimensions that are individually measured and then taken as a composite score for the GCI include Talent, Technology, and Tolerance.[72]

Assessing a nation's talent and technology seem logical, but what does tolerance have to do with the Global Creativity Index ranking? This measure analyzes how open it is to ethnic and religious minorities, and gay and lesbian people. This diversity aspect will be addressed later in the chapter, but a tolerance for all means more inputs and more ideas generated to solve problems. As noted earlier, allowing everyone to participate means everyone can contribute.

The United States fares well in the annual GCI report. In the 2015 study, the United States ranked second behind Australia in the overall ranking, and in the top five for Talent and Technology, while ranking 11th in the Tolerance category. Other countries that were ranked in the top ten include: Canada, Iceland, New Zealand, Denmark, Finland, Norway, Sweden, United Kingdom, Singapore, Germany, Japan, and Israel.[73]

---

72 The Global Creativity Index 2015, Martin Prosperity Index
73 Ibid.

Think Outside the Box

We often hear the term, "think outside the box," but in this case we are going to use a creativity exercise to illustrate the concept. You will need a blank paper (preferably an 8" by 11") and a pen or pencil for this exercise. Ruler would be handy. Take the blank paper, and place in a portrait position (shorter sides on top and bottom).

Keeping a one-inch margin, draw a rectangle box on the blank page. Should look like the following:

Next, draw 9 stars in the box. Three rows of 3 evenly across.

Here is the creativity challenge. Connect all nine stars drawing only three *straight* continuous lines. Put another way, you cannot pick up your pen or pencil if you are doing it right. You can't just draw a line from top to bottom across the three columns. When you finish, each star should be connected by a straight line.

Go ahead, try to solve this problem presented to you.

USING CREATIVITY TO SOLVE PROBLEMS

Creative Thinking

If you have not solved the creativity challenge, here are a couple of hints that might assist you.

- Ignore the rectangle box that you drew to start. If you drew it in pencil, erase it.
- Turn the entire page on its side, going from vertical look to a horizontal one.

The Solution

Turn the creativity test from a portrait position to a landscape one, in other words, turn it sideways.

Next, take your pen or pencil and start at the far upper left of the new orientation. Start drawing a sloping downward line by barely touching the very *top* of the first star in the first row. Continue the line through the middle of the second star, and then barely touch the bottom of the third star in the first row, going as far to the right of the page as you can. To draw this first straight line, notice that you are outside the margins of the original box frame that you drew.

For the second straight downward sloping line, you are doing the same but in reverse order (in a leftward direction). Start the second line by barely touching the very top of the far-right star of the second row. Continue the line through the middle of the second star, and then barely touch the bottom of the first star in the second row, going as far to the left of the page as you can.

By now, you should see the developing pattern. You are making a "Z" shape to connect all nine stars with only three straight lines. To successfully complete the exercise, you are repeating what you drew with the first straight line. Draw another downward sloping line, this time to the right. Again, the line barely touches the very top of the first star of the third row, continue through the middle of the second star, and finally barely touch the bottom of the last star on the third row.

Obstacles to Creative Thinking

Solving the problem, the way it was presented to you.

"Don't try to think outside the box – get outside the box, then think!"

Adam Hartung, Forbes columnist

Let's go back to the creativity challenge exercise. The way the problem was set up, a portrait orientation, would make it impossible to solve. Only when you turn the page sideways, a landscape orientation, could you have enough room to make the necessary "Z" formation. You also probably let the box frame that you drew limit your options. There was nothing that prevented you from going "outside the box."

As a leader, followers will routinely present a problem to you that needs a resolution. Do not fall into the trap that was demonstrated by the creativity exercise, by trying to solve the problem the exact way it was presented to you. Instead, challenge some of the assumptions being made. Ask questions. Sometimes those that are closest to the problem, cannot see what you might offer from an objective perspective.

Sticking with established patterns

"Creativity involves breaking out of established patterns in order to look at things in a different way."

Edward de Bono, physician and philosopher

I am certain that many of you originally drew the straight lines through the *middle* of each star. That would be the most traditional way of addressing this puzzle. However, to solve the three-line challenge, you needed to *barely* touch some of the stars, sometimes at the top or at the bottom.

Vertical Thinking can be the biggest barrier to creativity

I believe the biggest barrier to being creative is what I call vertical thinking. Based on the earlier obstacles, trying to solve the problem the way it was presented to you, and sticking with established patterns, we tend to move out too quickly. Our pattern goes like this:

A. Decide on one Course of Action
B. Action Step 1
C. Action Step 2
D. Action step 3

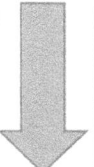

Vertical Thinking

The problem with going vertical thinking first, is that you already start down a path to solve a problem without exploring multiple options first. What are the chances that your chosen course of action, and the action steps to execute it, are the optimal solution?

Instead, I propose a better approach that I call going horizontal thinking. In this method, instead of A, B, C, D representing a single course of action followed by a handful of action steps, A, B, C, D represents going sideways first, horizontal, in seeking out multiple options before deciding on a course of action. This pattern would look different:

Option A   Option B   Option C   Option D

Horizontal Thinking

97

Going horizontal means looking at solving a problem in a variety of ways. I could go with Option A, perhaps the most obvious, and safest approach. On the other hand, I could consider Option B, a totally different approach. Then again, Option C is a hybrid approach, using a bit of Option A and some of Option B. Finally, Option D might be something totally untried before, and completely out-of-the-box.

The key to effective problem solving is developing multiple options, going horizontal. Once you've picked the best option, only then do you "go vertical" to execute the plan with the necessary and subsequent steps.

Fire and Ice

> "History, despite its wrenching pain, cannot be unlived, but if faced with courage, need not be lived again."
>
> *Maya Angelou, American poet*

We turn to two tragic incidents from the past to illustrate the notion of going horizontal first, in optimizing a solution to solve a problem. The first scenario is the Mann Gulch Fire, and the second is the more well-known *Titanic* disaster.

The Mann Gulch Fire

In 1805, when Lewis and Clark went on their historic expedition into the western part of the United States, they came upon a rugged and beautiful terrain that they would refer to as "the gates of the Rocky Mountains." This striking venue, along the upper Missouri River in Montana, became the backdrop of one of the more analyzed tragedies in fire science.

On August 5, 1949 a lightning strike sparked a wildfire to break out in the area known as Mann Gulch. On the scene, forest ranger James Harrison, a college student who worked during the summer, gallantly fought the fire by himself for four hours. Because of the inaccessible landscape, a team of smokejumpers presented the best option to fight the fire. Traveling in a C-47 aircraft, 15 firefighters, led by Wagner "Wag" Dodge parachuted into an open area at the top of the gulch.[74]

Upon landing, Dodge gave instructions for his crew to advance to the front of the fire. Later, he re-directed them to move down the gulch, flanking the fire. Dodge then broke off with Harrison, temporarily separated from the team. The two eventually went down the gulch to reunite with them.[75]

Down below, a rare but extremely dangerous "blow up" had occurred. The fire fighter term refers to a situation where the fire has suddenly intensified or spread rapidly, and a convergence of weather patterns and the hurricane type winds that big forest fires can spawn. At Mann Gulch, the extreme heat and high winds coming off the nearby river, pushed or "jumped" the fire from the south ridge to the northern slope. Seeing the fire rapidly spread upward across the dry grass, Dodge ordered his men to turn up the gulch, throwing away any heavy equipment that might slow their retreat.[76]

At this point, Dodge concluded that they could not outrun the quickly approaching forest fire to safety on the ridgeline. As the fire approached to within the length of a football field, Dodge came up with an idea that would save his life. He took a match and began a small fire in the grassy area, hoping that this "escape fire" would allow him and his men to lay down in the area until the main fire burned around them.[77]

Dodge motioned his men to join him in his unorthodox plan. In their mind, they were being directed from one raging fire chasing them, into another smaller one. A new concept, they did not fully understand that he was attempting to cross over the outside of the new

---
74 Forest History Society website, found at https://foresthistory.org/research-explore/us-forest-service-history/policy-and-law/fire-u-s-forest-service/famous-fires/mann-gulch-fire-1949/
75 Ibid.
76 Ibid.
77 Ibid.

fire into the *center* of the burnt-out area. As a result, they continued their fateful quest up the slope towards the higher ridge.[78]

Meanwhile, Dodge walked through the flames he had set, about thirty feet in. He continued to call his men to join him, but tragically, only two of them would find escape through another route, and 13 heroic firefighters lost their lives that day. Dodge survived with no injuries and his clothing intact.[79]

The Mann Gulch Fire: Vertical vs. Horizontal Thinking

My own son Jason is a firefighter, and I deeply respect all the brave men and women in that profession. The analysis of past decision-making is not to second-guess or to be critical by any means. Instead, we can use the lessons of history. In fact, the Board of Review for the Mann Gulch Fire recommended that future training include the use of escape-fire methods to avoid catastrophic fires, even if extremely rare.[80]

With the luxury of hindsight, we see the vertical thinking that took place in attempting to escape the ensuing fire.

- A. Course of Action: Avoid the fire
- B. Action Step 1: Drop equipment
- C. Action Step 2: Find escape route
- D. Action step 3: Outrun the fire

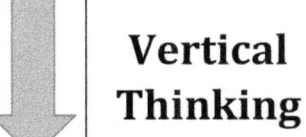

Vertical Thinking

Dodge, instead pursued a horizontal approach to the situation. There may have been other options in his mind, but for simplicity, we choose two.

---

78 Ibid.
79 Ibid.
80 Ibid.

Option A: Avoid the Fire   Option B: Build an Escape Fire

⟹

| Horizontal Thinking |

Wagner "Wag" Dodge's creativity did not prevent a tragic outcome to the disaster of the Mann Gulch Fire nearly 70 years ago. However, his innovation led to improved methods in firefighting that are leveraged today. We turn now to another disaster, the sinking of the Titanic. Unfortunately, the vertical thinking employed, without creative solutions, may have led to additional loss of lives.

The sinking of the *Titanic*

While many of you had not heard of the Mann Gulf Fire incident, everyone is familiar with the story of the *Titanic*. The *Titanic* was considered a modern marvel of its day. In 1911, the *Titanic's* hull, the watertight body of the ship, became at the time the world's largest moveable manmade object. By April 1912, the *Titanic* was ready for its maiden voyage from England to New York. On April 14, 1912 the *Titanic* collided with an iceberg in the North Atlantic Ocean, and sank less than three hours later, killing more than 1,500 of the 2,240 passengers.

In a *Harvard Business Review* article, "Find Innovation Where You Least Expect It, "Tony McCaffrey and Jim Pearson make the case that creativity and innovation could possibly have saved additional lives.[81] Let's look at the situation first from the traditional vertical approach.

---

81 Tony McCaffrey and Jim Pearson, "Find Innovation Where You Least Expect It," *Harvard Business Review*, December 2015

A. Course of Action: Put people in lifeboats
B. Action Step 1: Retrieve lifeboats
C. Action Step 2: Organize passengers
D. Action step 3: Lower lifeboats

As in the case of the review of the Mann Gulf Fire incident, my intent is to not second-guess the decisions of the Titanic's Captain and brave crew. They did the best they could under the dire circumstances, without the luxury of time. In addition to the lifeboat strategy, were there other options to consider? Could the crew have gone horizontal (multiple options) before pursuing the single course of action?

In the case of the *Titanic*, there were certainly additional resources for consideration beyond the obvious choice of lifeboats. On the *Titanic* itself, were the following means of survival:

- Car tires and inner tubes
- Steamer trunks
- Wooden tables
- Planks

Recall our earlier description of horizontal problem solving.

Option A: The most traditional approach to a problem
Option B: A different approach
Option C: A hybrid approach, using a bit of Option A and some of Option B
Option D: An untried solution, completely out-of-the box

In the case of the *Titanic*, we can now look at multiple options to keep people out of the water, the goal for survival.[82]

---

82 Ibid.

Option A: Place passengers in lifeboats
Option B: Use rubber tires (cars on board) and since wood floats (tables, doors, etc.)
Option C: Hybrid approach, build platforms between lifeboats
Option D: Use the iceberg (cold, but above the water)

The last option, somehow using the iceberg as a means of safety, completely goes against traditional thinking. Like the fire crew not entering Dodge's escape fire, seeing the iceberg as a potential solution is counterintuitive since it was the source of the problem in the first place.

Imagine, however, for a moment if the Captain of the *Titanic* visualized the iceberg, some 400 feet in length and rising high above the water, as a dry mountain. He, without hesitation, would direct lifeboats towards the object to keep passengers out of the frigid water until other ships arrived to rescue them. Not a long-term solution, just a temporary one. Since the terrain would be more difficult on the iceberg, perhaps the men who gave up their seats for the women and children could take a few lifeboats to see if this option worked. If it did, people could be dropped off on the iceberg, not tying up all the lifeboats.

Even the *Titanic* itself, although damaged had power to perhaps navigate towards the iceberg with many passengers still on board.

As McCaffrey and Pearson acknowledge in their *Harvard Business Review* article, options B, C, and D may not have worked on that cold, dark night. They do suggest, however, that innovative thinking seeks "the widest view" (horizontal thinking) to look beyond the obvious.[83]

Using Creativity in the Desert

During a deployment to the Kingdom of Saudi Arabia, as the senior financial manager deployed for the Air Force, I faced a problem that took some creative thinking to solve. In 1991, the United Nations Security Council passed a resolution that Saddam Hussein cease

---

83 Ibid.

repression of his civilian population that included attacks against the Shi'ite Muslims in southern Iraq.

In 1992, President Bush initiated surveillance operations to ensure Hussein's compliance with the United Nations. The coalition of U.N. forces enforced a "no fly" zone that barred Iraq's military from flying over the surveillance area. As a result, Operation Southern Watch became the means to enforce the restriction.

After a terrorist bombing in June 1996 at the Khobar Towers in Saudi Arabia, the Air Force relocated Southern Watch operations to Prince Sultan Air Base (PSAB) for additional force protection, south of the capital Riyadh. In April 1998, I arrived at PSAB for a six-month tour as the Comptroller.

Part of my responsibilities included a two-person Disbursing Agent function for the entire Southwest Asia Theater to include Saudi Arabia, Kuwait, Oman, and the United Arab Emirates. The Disbursing Agent operated essentially as the important banking operation, by coordinating with seven Paying Agents across the region. Because of the earlier terrorist bombing, those of us assigned to the Prince Sultan Air Base were very limited in our travels. We needed permission directly from the Vice-Commander to venture off the base.

Despite these obstacles, the Disbursing Agent used aircraft flying back and forth from our Saudi installation to the other sites in theater to ensure smooth operations across the multiple Paying Agents. One night, the Disbursing Agent (a Lieutenant) woke me up in my tent. "Sir," he started, "We have a big problem." He went on to explain that a political decision abruptly stopped these flights.

To the rest of the nearly 5,000 Airmen at Prince Sultan Air Base, no ramifications existed. Our patrol missions, along with those from the French and British forces, would continue. Only my Disbursing Agent had a function that reached across the region, and therefore affected negatively.

We immediately called the Air Force Base back in the United States responsible for supporting our deployment to inform them of the situation. They in turn, raised the issue up through the chain-of-command for visibility and a potential resolution to a difficult problem.

In short order, we had a few recommendations. The first, see if we could use commercial aircraft that occasionally flew delivery missions for the government. The second option presented was to shut down the overseas Disbursing Agent function. In my mind, these were not valid options.

One day, I looked at an increasingly anxious Lieutenant Disbursing Agent and came up with an out-of-the-box creative idea. The political choice meant that no flights could *originate* from Saudi Arabia to the other countries in theater. There was no concern if flights went to those sites from *another* location, just other than Saudi Arabia.

I continued with my idea. Suppose we found a way to move the Disbursing Agent function from Prince Sultan Air Base to a place where there were missions that went to our Paying Agents in the other countries. The answer: Ramstein Air Base, Germany. Five years earlier, I was the Accounting and Finance Officer at that installation, the largest in Europe.

I convinced the Vice Commander to allow myself and the Lieutenant to take a military flight to Ramstein to explore the logistics. The first hurdle was to see if there were regular flights from Ramstein to the other bases. Fortunately, they served as an operational hub and had no problem with our Disbursing Agent joining the missions. Next, I met with my old office and the new Finance Officer to ask for small space for the two-person Disbursing function and minimal administrative support. Again, we gained support without any issues. So far so good.

Next, we visited a German friend in Frankfurt from my prior experience as the Ramstein Finance Officer, to establish the necessary banking relationship. Within a short time, we worked out the arrangements and another hurdle cleared. In fact, we now had access to a remarkable "financial hub" in Frankfurt that would dramatically improve the Disbursing Agent function, including electronic transfers instead of hard cash.

When we arrived back in Saudi Arabia, we contacted the home

base back in the states, filled with good news on our highly productive trip. Surprisingly, they did not initially support our idea. They raised concerns on how it would look that the Disbursing Agent function for all Air Force personnel deployed in the Middle East were "drinking beers" in Germany. My Lieutenant took that as a personal insult.

In the end, after some tough negotiation, we prevailed and moved the Disbursing Agent from my Comptroller office in Saudi Arabia to Ramstein Air Base, Germany. We tapped into much improved operational and financial hubs and provided better support to our deployed troops in the theater. On a personal note, I was later recognized as the military's Comptroller of the Year, a prestigious award.

Diversity and Creativity

> "The best way to have a good idea is to have a lot of ideas."
>
> *Linus Pauling,*
> *American chemist and educator*

At this point, you may be thinking to yourself, "I understand the concept of being creative and seeking multiple options before deciding on a final solution, but I'm not a creative type." Do not despair; there is still a way as a leader to produce creative ideas. The answer is to leverage diversity.

> "Diversity and inclusion must go hand-in-hand to drive results...research bolsters the case that employers who build diverse and inclusive teams see the best outcomes."[84]
>
> *Laura Sherbin, CFO and Director of Research*
> *at the Center for Talent Innovation*

---

84 Erik Larson, "New Research: Diversity + Inclusion = Better Decision Making At Work", *Forbes*, September 21, 2017

It turns out, diversity and inclusion are not just a "nice to have," it is a "must have" for economic success. In a *Forbes* magazine article entitled, "New Research: Diversity + Inclusion = Better Decision Making at Work," Erik Larson sums up the case for a leader ensuring all members of the organization are participating.[85]

Forbes did research into inclusive decision-making to better understand how much improvement is possible with diversity and inclusion. The two-year study looked at approximately 600 business decisions made by 200 different business teams across a wide spectrum of companies. The bottom line to the research showed that there was a linkage between better business performance and inclusive decision-making. The study found that decision-making improves as the diversity of the team increases. Inclusive teams make better business decisions up to 87 percent of the time.[86]

A University of Michigan professor Scott Page, in his book *The Difference*, concluded with evidence that diverse groups made better decisions over the long-run then individuals alone or homogenous groups. More importantly, this conclusion held true no matter how brilliant or smart the individuals or members of the homogenous groups. In other words, being the "smartest guy or gal in the room" is not going to take you very far.[87]

In their book, *Strengths Based Leadership: Great Leaders, Teams, and Why People Follow*, Tom Rath and Barry Conchie further validate the importance of diversity and inclusion. Their own studies show that teams composed of individuals who tend to look at issues in the same way, possess similar educational background, with similar experience and approaches, are not the recipe for success. They discovered that engaged teams welcome diversity to include differences in race, gender, and age. Disengaged teams tend to do the opposite.[88]

---

85   Ibid.
86   Ibid.
87   Scott Page, *The Difference: How the Power of Diversity Creates Better Groups, Firms, Schools, and Societies* (Princeton: Princeton University Press, 2007)
88   Tom Rath and Barry Conchie, *Strengths Based Leadership: Great Leaders, Teams, and Why People Follow* (Omaha: Gallup Press, 2008), 74.

Final thoughts on the value of Diversity and Creativity

> "An organization simply cannot be exceptional if people don't speak up and candidly share what they see, think, and believe. Otherwise, ideas are left inside people's minds instead of out on the table, available for dissection and exploration. Creative problem-solving suffers..."[89]
>
> *John G. Miller, author*

As a new leader, seek out and embrace diversity on your team. Remember, principle six is that a complete leader leads *all* people. Diversity is more than just differences in what we can see. It can include diversity of thought. A leader needs to leverage individual differences and harvest them into team strength. Leaving anyone from participating means that not everyone is contributing. Those contributions include proposing creative and innovative ideas to problems that you and the organization will surely face.

---

[89]

CHAPTER 8

Knowledge is on a learning curve, character on a straight line

"The function of education is to teach one to think intensively and to think critically. Intelligence plus character – that is the goal of true education."

Martin Luther King, Jr., American minister and civil rights leader

AS A NEW college graduate, you have advanced your knowledge, most likely in an area like business, engineering, or social work. At some schools, there is an additional emphasis on character development. I witnessed these programs at both the Air Force Academy and The Citadel, The Military College of South Carolina. The cadet honor code means a student who lies, steals, cheats, or even tolerates those behaviors, faces discipline up to and including dismissal. I am proud to have been an adjunct instructor at both institutions.

While more schools are emphasizing character development in the core curriculum, most courses do not explicitly incorporate the importance of integrity and character. The National Soft Skills Association believes that educational institutions emphasize technical knowledge but emphasize less the necessary soft skills that employers are demanding. One conclusion might be that these soft skills are not taught because there is an assumption that somehow students already have them.[90] As a result, you may not fully understand the relevance of character, compared to the technical skills acquired through your education.

Yet, in a study of engineering education conducted 100 years ago by the Carnegie Foundation for the Advancement of Teaching, in a survey of 30,000 members of engineering societies, the number one quality they felt needed for top engineers was character.[91]

Competence *and* Character

In his book *Principle-Centered Leadership*, Dr. Stephen R. Covey emphasizes that for someone to be trustworthy, the foundation of trust, they must possess *both* competence and character. Dr. Covey states, "If one is incompetent, training and development can help. But if one has a character flaw, he or she must make and keep promises... to rebuild relationships of trust."[92]

The ability to trust each other, to be honest, and to place others before self is the cornerstone of the business world you are entering. Ed Fuller, President of Marriott Lodging International, once observed, "Honesty is not just the best policy in business, it's also the only policy that provides any assurance that the people with whom you have relationships will be honest with you."[93]

In the chart below, we see that over time, we gain knowledge in the classroom.

---

90 National soft skills association, website found at https://www.nationalsoftskills.org/
91 Found at website, http://www.nationalsoftskills.org/downloads/Mann-1918-Study_of_Engineering_Educ.pdf
92 Stephen Covey, *Principle-Centered Leadership* (New York: Simon & Schuster, 1990)
93 Ed Duller, *You Can't Lead With Your Feet On the Desk: Building Relationships, Breaking Down Barriers, and Delivering Profits* (Hoboken: John Wiley and Sons Publishing, 2010)

KNOWLEDGE IS ON A LEARNING CURVE, CHARACTER ON A STRAIGHT LINE

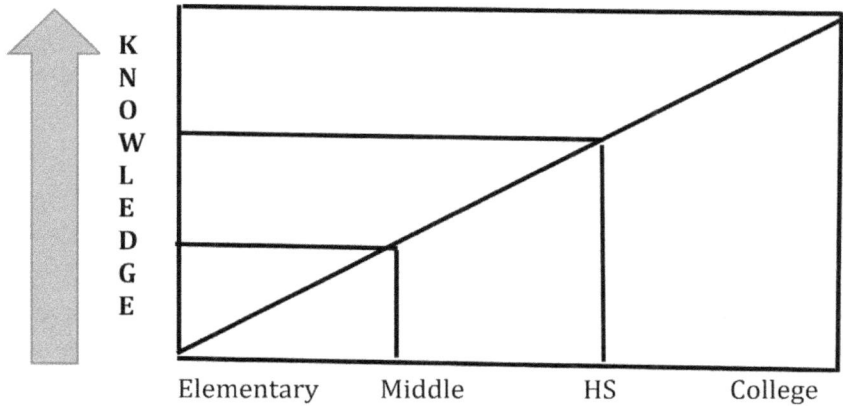

As a student progresses through the education system, his or her general knowledge increases accordingly. Someone attending college is sure to know more than one in middle school or high school. Their brains are more developed, and the years at school stretch their learning capacity. However, character should not be on an upward sloping line as general knowledge is. It should instead be on a straight line – constant.

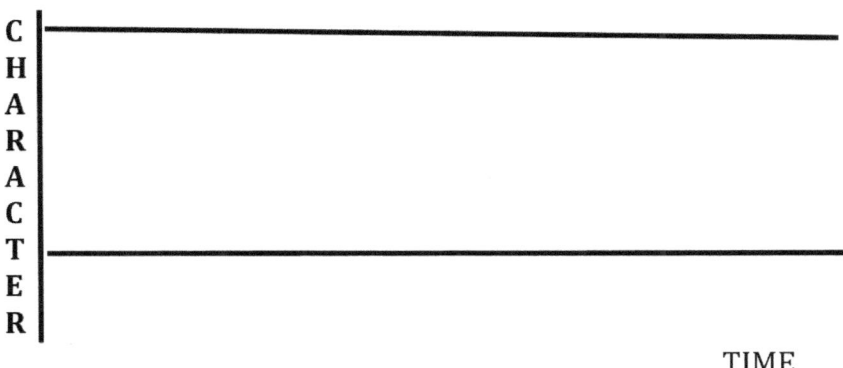

Similarly, as a college graduate, your employer will be patience as you learn the tools of your profession. Over time, you will get better at your job through experience. However, the same employer does not expect to teach you basic integrity and ethical values. You should enter the workforce with an elevated level of character, and that level should remain high throughout your career. On a straight line, not upward slope.

What is on the inside is more important than the outside

> "I have a dream that my four little children will one day live in a nation where they will not be judged by the color of their skin, but by the content of their character."
>
> *Martin Luther King, Jr. (from the I have a dream speech in Washington, D.C.)*

The inner core of a person, character, is more important than visible attributes. Former Secretary of Defense Robert Gates told a graduating class at the United States Naval Academy the following advice:

> "Nowadays it seems like integrity – or honor or character – is kind of quaint, a curious, old-fashioned notion...But for a real leader, personal virtues – self-reliance, self-control, honor, truthfulness, morality – are absolute. These are the building blocks of character, of integrity – and only on that foundation can real leadership be built."[94]

---

94 *Washington Post*, The Fed Page, May 30, 2011

Parting advice on character

"Be more concerned with your character than your reputation, because your character is what you really are, while your reputation is merely what others think you are."[95]

John Wooden, national champion coach

Like it or not, as a new graduate, you will be in the spotlight for others to judge your actions as well as your words. Do not impair your influence and authority through negative activities. Always do the right thing, even when no one is looking. Character is extremely important.

---

95 Found at website Brainy Quote https://www.brainyquote.com/quotes/john_wooden_163015

CHAPTER 9

Lane Management

> "I've always operated so far outside my lane, I'm not sure what lane is mine anymore."
>
> *General Michael T. Flynn*

MOST ANYONE WHO swims regularly will understand the basics of swim lane management. Whether at a community pool doing laps, or at a team practice, the swim lane etiquette allows a pool to be maximized when there are not enough lanes for only one swimmer per lane. These rules include the following guidelines:[96]

- Always let the other person swimming know you are entering the pool
- Do not start or turn in front of faster swimmers
- Take note of swim speed before you enter and use a lane appropriate to your speed
- Tap feet to pass a slower swimmer
- Faster swimmers should have right of way
- Don't use wide strokes when others are using long strokes

---

[96] 3 SWIM ETIQUETTE Mistakes That Are MAKING YOU SLOWER, found on You Tube, Triathlon Taren presenter

To further assist with maximizing performance, there are swim lane lines. These lines, made up of individual floats, do more than just keep swimmers in their respective lane. For example, a coach can set up a color scheme so that the last part of the floats is all red, indicating to the swimmers that they are nearing the end of the lane.[97]

As you enter or progress in the workplace after completing your college degree, there are no designated swim lanes or swim lines that will similarly guide you. The purpose of this chapter is to offer some useful tips on working with others on the same team. Not only interactions with your boss or followers that we have emphasized in previous chapters, but also your equals, your peers, and your teammates. This horizontal dimension can be the most difficult because there are no clear boundaries or etiquette as found in the swimming pool.

There may not be an "I" in team, but there is a "ME."

> "Individual commitment to a group effort -- that is what makes a team work, a company work, a society work, a civilization work."
>
> *Renowned football coach Vince Lombardi*

Up to this point, a new college graduate has relied primarily on himself or herself for success. No one escorted you to get to your class on time, did your homework, prepared for and took your exams, and so on. For the most part, college life is an individual "sport." When your graduation cap, after being thrown high in the air, falls to the ground, that begins to change. You need to now think of the organization first, ahead of yourself.

This transition may not be an easy one for you. Again, there has been a direct correlation between your personal efforts and your achievement. Work hard, get good grades, earn recognition (top ranking in your class, honor societies, etc.). What is important in the

---

97 Found at website https://www.swimoutlet.com/guides/how-to-choose-lane-lines

workplace, however, is organizational success. That is why employers look for employees to show empathy toward one's colleagues, as listed as a top skill in Google's Project Oxygen (mentioned in the introduction chapter). Your team first approach will ultimately pay dividends over a me first approach.

In his book, *Leading the Charge: Leadership Lessons from the Battlefield to the Boardroom*, General Tony Zinni shares what he called one of his greatest leadership moments regarding individual achievement versus organizational success.[98]

As one of ten company commanders in the battalion, his performance would be judged against the nine other Captains. As General Zinni recounts the situation, the battalion commander had an obvious favorite among the subordinate company commanders. He would even go so far as to say how much this one Captain reminded him of himself at his age.[99]

When it came time to receive his formal evaluation, Zinni was shocked that he had been chosen over the favored Captain and rated number one. With a look of surprise on his face, the battalion commander asked what was wrong. Zinni honestly replied that he thought the other Captain that had been regularly and publicly praised would surely be ranked number one among the ten company commanders.[100]

The battalion commander's words to then Captain Zinni made a lasting impression on him: "He (the other Captain) is a great individual leader, probably the best in the battalion, in my opinion, but your company was superior. My judgment is based on performance of the organization you lead. Whatever you're doing works."[101]

Captain Zinni went on to become 4-star General Zinni, Commander-in-Charge of the critical Central Command. He learned a valuable lesson from his boss that he would be judged primarily on

---

98 Tony Zinni and Tony Koltz, *Leading the Charge: Leadership Lessons from the Battlefield to the Boardroom* (New York: Palgrave MacMillan, 2009)
99 Ibid.
100 Ibid.
101 Ibid.

the performance of his organization that he led, not necessarily his own personal leadership traits -- a big difference.[102]

Partner with rather than compete with your teammates

One of the golden rules of followership is to not let your boss look bad because of your actions or inactions. Similarly, a golden rule involving your teammates is to never try to look good by making or allowing others to look bad. This is not a zero-sum game. If a teammate fails, the entire group is a failure. Consider your peers as business partners, not competitors. If you are in business with someone, a partner, you will look at their success as your success, and they will do the same with you. Why would I want to hurt our business interests by allowing my partner to come up short?

In the same manner, your boss will be looking for who has what I call *leadership maturity*. Many leaders can lead their own team quite well, but it takes a special kind of maturity for someone to defer to the greater good of the organization. If you see a peer struggling, offer to help in any way you can. Do so without telling the boss to earn special recognition or praise that only diminishes the teammate.

Do not worry who gets credit. If you came up with an idea that others could advance the mission forward, it will eventually come out whose initiative it was in the first place. Let those things come naturally. You do not have to force it. As President Harry Truman observed, "It is amazing what you can accomplish if you do not care who gets the credit."[103]

I have also learned that it is important to bring along your teammates early in the process if you are thinking of doing something different in your area of responsibility. The worst thing that can happen is if you spring an initiative on your boss and he or she asks if you have considered the impact on other areas. What is music to a supervisor's

---

102 Ibid.
103 Found at website Brainy Quote https://www.brainyquote.com/quotes/harry_s_truman_109615

ears is when you can say that you ran it by another department, and you have already addressed their initial concerns. Remember, your boss does not want to approve new ideas that could be risky to their own reputation. By involving others, and bringing them in early, you are reducing the amount of risk and therefore improving your supervisor's support and enthusiasm.

Meet regularly with your peers

One way to avoid encroaching on another person's lane is to meet regularly with your peers, especially those that you interact with routinely to meet mission objectives. When I worked for the Department of Agriculture (Food Safety), I initiated a bi-weekly lunch meeting with two senior colleagues, the Chief Information Officer (CIO) and the Associate Administrator for the Office of Management. Not only did we share what was happening in our own areas, these meetings allowed us time to develop the personal side of our relationship beyond work. You are more likely to get cooperation from others if there is some type of bond or friendship that you can call on to get things done.

In an earlier case, when I arrived in New Orleans, Louisiana as the "Katrina CFO" for the Gulf Coast Recovery Office, I quickly hired new Finance Directors to lead financial management operations in Louisiana, Mississippi, and Alabama. The Texas operation had a Comptroller already in place who was part of the FEMA cadre who routinely responded to natural disaster relief.

Early on, we gathered in Mobile, Alabama as a central meeting point to get on the same page (lane assignments) to advance the long-term recovery mission. Theresa Nola, the Alabama Finance Director, would drive down a couple of hours from Montgomery, Alabama. Edward Troy, the Louisiana Finance Director, would join us from about the same distance from New Orleans. Greg James, the Mississippi Finance Director, would drive the shorter hour ride from Biloxi, Mississippi. Finally, Ann Udland, the Texas Comptroller would call in and graciously endure our give-and-take strategy sessions for a couple of hours. As a member of the seasoned Comptroller Cadre, she provided us "rookies" her sage wisdom and advice, as did other FEMA Comptrollers.

Together, our group knew that our mission would be profoundly different. My new team and I faced different challenges associated with the long-term recovery effort from Hurricanes Katrina and Rita not found in most of the disasters. We felt that we had two sets of customers. The first set was the disaster survivors and the local governments, who needed assistance in rebuilding their lives and communities,

We also saw the American public as a second set of customers who trusted us to be good stewards of their hard-earned taxes. We knew the notion of looking at cost controls and fiscal discipline were not always going to be a top priority for a culture bent on quick response. In fact, many people used to the old way of doing business would push us back. After Katrina, however, there was a call for a "new FEMA" – one that sought better business practices and to instill public confidence.

With the FEMA mission squarely in mind, we spent hours of hearty discussion among ourselves. When we were done, we had written on sheets of paper what we felt our own mission would be in Gulf Coast financial management for the next several years. We committed that we would produce annual budgets and establish internal controls in the Katrina recovery phase – a first for FEMA.

After this initial meeting, we would continue to meet in Mobile to stay connected, despite our geographical separation from each other. We held regular conference calls as well. In my mind, our group needed to always speak with one voice and one set of values. If Edward (Louisiana Finance Director), for example, held firm on a request for funding that he thought was inappropriate, and Greg or Theresa in Mississippi or Alabama approved a similar request, the differences would be exploited, and we would lose our desired budgetary and internal controls.

To gain support of the program directors, I established a Good

Stewardship Council. The Council came together to collaborate efforts across the Gulf Coast Recovery area. Before long, even senior officials from FEMA headquarters in Washington, D.C, started flying down to attend our meetings in New Orleans and later in Mobile.

In the end, our efforts paid off. Our group won the first ever Department of Homeland Security Chief Financial Officer Award in the Planning, Budget, and Evaluation category. More importantly, we met our goal of supporting the recovery mission in the Gulf Coast while being good stewards of all taxpayer provided resources. As a leader, I encouraged that we had proper lane management, swimming all in the same direction and coordinated.

Final thoughts on Lane Management

"A rising tide lifts all boats."

Our first chapter emphasized the principle of good followership. In this chapter, we highlighted the importance of being a good teammate, especially to your peer group. Just as there is swim lane etiquette to maximize pool performance, we discussed ways to optimize organizational performance by working well with your teammates. Do not ignore this important principle. Your boss will appreciate your leadership maturity, your peers will respect your willingness to inform and engage them, and in the end, all players will benefit from a team first approach.

CHAPTER **10**

Using the APE theory

"Charles was a changed chimp. Sure, being a CEO would mean encountering some difficulties, but he now fully enjoyed his career and life in general. On that fateful day that seemed like only yesterday, Gregory and the other gorillas like Gil and Kayla had taught Charles many lessons."[104]

From the book, Leading in the Jungle

Gorilla Meets Chimp

In my last leadership book, entitled *Leading in the Jungle: A Fable of a Chimp's Quest to Lead like a Gorilla*, I share an amusing and insightful fable of a chimp's lofty quest to lead like a gorilla as he embarks on an unforgettable journey through a forest filled with powerful leadership lessons.

After yet another draining staff meeting, frustrations and insecurities about his own leadership as a Chimp Executive Officer (CEO), Charles wanders off and eventually ends up in North Forest. After he is welcomed by both the gorilla community and Gregory, their wise silverback leader, Charles begins observing, reflecting, and learning

---
[104] Joseph Garcia, *Leading in the Jungle: a fable of a chimp's quest to lead like a gorilla* (Bloomington: Abbott Press, 2014)

not only from the gorillas, but also from the events taking place around him.

While discovering how to lead more deliberatively, demonstrate accountability, and ask the right questions, Charles encounters a branch chief, pumps wood at the fitness center, and learns how a neighboring tribe of elephants managed to partner with the gorilla community.

The Alpha Ape's Final Advice
An excerpt from the end of the *Leading in the Jungle* book: [105]

Gregory took a deep breath. "Charles, I am not very good at saying good-bye, so this may get clumsy."

The chimp looked up. "I know what you mean."

"I enjoyed our time together, Charles. I never had a brother growing up...it is a long story...but somehow, I view you more than a new friend. I learned a lot from you today."

Charles replied, "I was the student today. I cannot tell you how much I've tried to take in from all the experiences of the day. Thank you for graciously allowing me to be a bystander. My only regret is that I did not write down some of my observations so I could remember them, when I get back. I will never be able to recollect all the key lessons."[106]

Gregory paused for a moment and then looked around. He found a twig and then returned to where Charles was standing. "Charles, you realize that gorillas and chimpanzees may be different in size, but we come from the same ape family." Gregory leaned over and began writing on the ground near the pond. When he was finished, he spoke softly to Charles.

---

105 Ibid.
106 Ibid.

"A simple way I remember how to lead is APE."

Charles leaned over to see what the alpha ape had written on the ground.[107]

Accountable
Partner
Everyone

Gregory gave Charles a moment before proceeding. "I am accountable for my actions. It starts with me to do the right thing. Never go it alone. Always partner with others. Finally, everyone is important and can make a difference. You see. APE," said Gregory.[108]

This tenth and final principle, *Using the APE theory*, in many ways effectively captures many of the earlier concepts we covered throughout this book. We will review each element of the APE theory, a powerful tool for a new college graduate.

Be Accountable for your words and actions

The only time a leader should say "I" is to pronounce "I messed up" or "I assume full responsibility." Otherwise, it should be "we," which demonstrates a team approach. Do not be concerned with covering up your mistakes. Your peers and followers understand that you are human, and a leadership role is not easy. When you continue to deny or deflect responsibility when mistakes happen, you only lose credibility along the way. Instead of appearing big, a leader diminishes in stature.

Years ago, I served as the Chief Financial Officer for the Food Safety Inspection Services Agency in Washington, D.C., part of the Department of Agriculture. Those years were especially challenging with the fiscal uncertainty and austerity that came with the budget

---
107 Ibid.
108 Ibid.

cuts known as sequestration.

On one occasion, I provided less than accurate budget information to the agency's administrator during one of our weekly private meetings. Frankly, I had gotten ahead of my staff that had earlier provided me some preliminary numbers. They also cautioned me that they were still running through the necessary calculations before reaching a final figure. I provided the budget numbers anyway without waiting.

This was an unforced error on my part. In addition to providing poor advice to the administrator, I also made the budget staff look bad. When the updated budget-related calculation was finally ready, it was significantly off from my earlier estimate. At this point, I could let it go and provide the new information to my boss over time to minimize my mistake. However, that would be unfair to both him and my staff.

I quickly arranged for a second meeting with the administrator, but I invited the two senior budget directors to the meeting as well. In my boss' office, I told him that it was my fault, not my staff, for prematurely providing important budgetary information. I apologized to him and my team and promised to do better in the future. Fortunately, my boss was gracious in his response, as was the budget crew.

Demonstrating accountability is often difficult but necessary as a leader. As you start your career, recognize that like character, accountability should *not* be on a learning curve that you strive to get better over time.

Avoid putting up a Failure Wall

Firewall

When assigned as the Vice President for Finance and Business at The Citadel, The Military College of South Carolina, a severe fire broke out in our Beach House. The Beach House (or Beach Club) provided an excellent venue for weddings and receptions, or frequent gatherings of employees enjoying time on the beach around Charleston, South Carolina.

Fortunately, the resident occupants escaped without bodily injury, but they did lose much of their possessions. It would take months for the facility to reopen. In a conversation with one of the fire crew that had bravely fought and put out the fire, he showed me the firewall that had effectively saved complete destruction. The firewall did its job, by providing a separation from the residence side to the main part of the structure that prevented the fire from immediately spreading further. This allowed enough time for the fire crews to contain the fire.

In short, a firewall is a good thing. It contains the spread of fire.

Failure wall

"If you take personal ownership…research shows you're much more likely to learn from and work harder after that mistake."[109]

On the other hand, a failure wall prevents a leader from accepting responsibility and learning from mistakes. Unlike a firewall, it is not a good thing. We can visually depict a failure wall in the following manner.

---
109 Gretchen Gavett,"When We Learn From Failure (and When We Don't," *Harvard Business Review*, May 2014

While you want a fire to stay behind the firewall, you do not need a wall that presents failure from reaching you, which is harmful. For most of us, our ego will prevent us from acknowledging when we have failed. No one likes to look less than successful. Because of this innate quality, you will do yourself a big favor if you graciously accept constructive criticism and feedback when provided to you.

My experience with a Failure Wall

Early in my military time, a Lieutenant Colonel greatly influenced my career trajectory. I was assigned to the United States Air Force Academy, not as a cadet, but a newly promoted staff sergeant (enlisted person) working in the Finance Office. After two years on station, I noticed that every quarter, there would be formal recognition for the top performers.

After one awards ceremony, I realized that I had not even been nominated for the award, let alone recognized with one. I went home that evening and wrote down all my accomplishments that I felt warranted a nomination. The next day I went in to see the Lieutenant Colonel in charge of the organization.

At first, the officer patiently listened to my ramblings about how I was making such great contributions to the mission and that I felt slighted by not been nominated as many of my peers had been. When I was done, he politely said that it was not up to him to nominate me, and that I would have to take up the issue with my immediate supervisor, a senior non-commissioned officer at the time. Although he was technically correct, I did not let it go and continued to press him for justice.

After a while, it was as if the officer took off his rank. He looked me in the eye and in a "man-to-man" tone, told me how he really felt about my complaint. He told me that his perception of me was in fact not in harmony what I thought of myself. The Colonel pointed out that my uniform could look better, my military bearing needed improvement, and he offered a few other candid observations.

Stunned, I did not see this side of the conversation coming. Rather than agreeing with me and handing me some type of trophy from his desk, he articulated areas of improvement instead.

Here is where the failure wall almost got me. For the next day or two, I sulked about my situation. How could that Colonel be so wrong? Didn't he see all the great things that I was doing? About the third day, I looked at myself in the mirror. I reflected on what the Colonel had told me. Maybe he was not totally correct in his assessment, but he had given me enough to think about. After all, you do not reach that high a rank without some insight. I removed the failure wall and let the constructive criticism in.

I made the necessary changes. I bought new uniforms and had them tailored for a good fit. I began to act more professional with my own troops and tried to be a better supervisor. These little things made a difference because within a year, not only was I selected as performer of the quarter, but eventually performer of the year. That one award became critical since I used it in my application to attend a commissioning program. Twenty years, I attained the rank of, ironically enough, Lieutenant Colonel.

Someone had the moral courage to provide it to my straight. Seek others who will do likewise. Personal accountability is essential to professional growth.

Accepting Failure sparks Creativity

Another benefit of not putting a failure wall up between you and your mistakes is that if you are less worried about criticism, you are more likely to seek innovative options that might not always work. Remember, 60 percent of the hiring managers felt that new graduates lacked the proper critical thinking and problem-solving skills to enter the workforce. The seventh principle, using creativity to solve problems, addressed this gap.

In a recent article in *Trusteeship* magazine, produced by the Association of Governing Boards (AGB) of Universities and Colleges, the AGB Board issue a statement on innovation in higher education that included the following:

> "In this new setting, a culture of innovation prizes and rewards creative thinking. It empowers constituents – staff, faculty, administration, students, and community members – to think creatively about solutions and to implement them. It also embraces risk and failure as integral aspects of innovation. It even rewards failures following good attempts – 'shots on goal' – to motivate the continued effort to develop new ideas."[110]

Do not let the paralysis of fearing failure, by building and keeping a failure wall up around you, inhibit the learning from your occasional misstep. Never seek to fail, but always be open to learn from it.

Always Partner with Others

> "If you in any way hinder the bigger team – your organization – because of your desire to achieve personal success or even success of your department, then you may need to take steps back to keep the team's mission in hand."[111]
>
> *John Maxwell, leadership author*

Our ninth principle, (lane management) emphasized the importance of a new college graduate to partner with rather than compete with your teammates. Never go it alone. Years ago, I had the privilege of meeting a real American hero who demonstrated the importance of working together as a team.

While assigned a second time to the Air Force Academy, this time as an officer, the city of Colorado Springs decided to partner with the military installations in the area including the Academy and Fort Carson

---

[110] From *AGB Board of Directors' Statement on Innovation in Higher Education* (2017)

[111] John Maxwell, *The 17 Essential Qualities of a Team Player: Becoming the Kind of Person Every Team Wants* (Nashville: Thomas Nelson publishing, 2002), 94-95.

army base, to promote the upcoming Hispanic Heritage Month activities. We formed a joint committee, and I was the Air Force Academy representative. By partnering, we were able to combine our resources and hold one large event, instead of three smaller ones.

One of the primary tasks of the committee was to choose the appropriate keynote speaker. After careful deliberation, we were able to select a real American hero, Roy Benavidez, Master Sergeant, U.S. Army, retired. A Medal of Honor recipient, he even has a GI Joe action figure made after him. I was given the honor by the committee of serving as the host and escort for Sergeant Benavidez during his visit to Colorado Springs from his home in Texas. When I met him at the airport, as I shook his hands, I noticed the scars and other signs of hand-to-hand combat that represented great personal sacrifice to his nation.

For the next several days, I spent time with Roy, inviting him to the house for supper, spending time with him in his billeting room, and just enjoying his company. He had recently written his book, *Medal of Honor: A Vietnam Warrior's Story*, so I arranged for a book-signing event at one of the local bookstores. Despite running him ragged, I asked Sergeant Benavidez if he would speak to my leadership class and he graciously agreed to do so.

Roy made sure that I always referred to him as a Medal of Honor recipient – not winner. As he joked, "This isn't a prize you win at a raffle, you have to earn it." As I also learned, he was entitled to some unique protocol privileges. Even though he retired at the rank of Master Sergeant, he stayed in the finest Academy Distinguished Visitors quarters. We were assigned a staff car that I used to escort him around the Academy.

Although these perks were impressive, there was one form of protocol that I thought outweighed all the others. As a Medal of Honor recipient, all military persons were to salute him, regardless of their rank (including officers).

Before visiting my class, The Academy Superintendent and Commandant of Cadets, both general officers, expressed interest in visiting with him and thanking him for speaking to several cadet groups. As I escorted the aging warrior to the front office, I saw that the Commandant was waiting for us outside in the hallway.

When we approached, the general snapped to attention, and smartly saluted Sergeant Benavidez. I must admit it was a special moment to watch but Roy just took it all in stride.

When I found out that Sergeant Benavidez would be our guest, I assigned a special project to the leadership class. The cadets were reading a book on the Vietnam conflict. To honor Roy's service during that war, where he had earned his Medal of Honor, the cadets gave small group re-enactment from a segment in the book. They then explained the leadership implication or lesson for them.

Roy seemed to really enjoy himself, and the cadets, as always did a magnificent job. Some dressed up in camouflage uniforms, wore paint on their faces, and obtained helmets and wooden rifles for their role-playing. I had obtained access to a large venue, not our normal classroom that made it more intimate and special.

After the group presentations, we had just a few minutes left but I wanted to give the class a chance to speak to a real American hero and ask a few questions. As they arranged their chairs to face Sergeant Benavidez, I could see the cadets were enthralled with the moment. When they settled, I chose one of the cadets, out of many, who had raised their hand to ask a question.

It was a simple question, but a powerful one. "Sir," the cadet started, "Why did you do it?" The cadet was referring to the Medal of Honor citation that documented Roy's incredible feat. I was also fortunate to find a rare clip in the Academy library, of President Reagan, reading the entire citation himself before presenting Roy his medal. The video was shown to them at the beginning of the class before Roy and I arrived. Why had he risked his life so many times that fateful day in Vietnam?

Before I share his answer, let's review what he could have said. Roy's call sign was "Tango-Mike-Mike." That stood for That Mean Mexican. Roy had grown up in tough barrios and had to defend himself, sometimes from racial prejudice (being part Indian and part Mexican). He, therefore, could have replied that he did it because he was one mean hombre.

Instead, Sergeant Benavidez did not say anything bravado or cocky, or even about himself at all. He answered the cadet's simple question with a simple answer.

"I did it for my unit. I did it for my team."

Roy had gone through what he would call "six hours of hell" for his team. He kept being shot and stabbed by the enemy, but he kept fighting on to lift his teammates' spirits and rally them to persevere.

If the power of the team can motivate a person to sacrifice his life for them, surely we can do our part to advance our organization's mission, goals, and objectives, and be a willing partner and teammate.

Everyone is Important

Principle six emphasized diversity, and how a complete leader needs to lead all people. Every single person can contribute to your success if you allow him or her to participate. We turn again to the lessons of history. This time to show the differences between an egotistical leader who does not embrace diversity and a total team approach, and someone who leverages these traits for success.

The Battle of Little Bighorn

On June 25, 1876, the American military suffered what many experts consider the worst single defeat in our history, the decimation of the entire Seventh Calvary. It was called the Battle of the Little Bighorn. In his book, *The Genius of Sitting Bull*, author Emmett C. Murphy describes the differences between the two leaders involved; victorious leader of the Sioux nation Chief Sitting Bull and the defeated General George Custer.[112]

Murphy depicts the General as an arrogant, egotistical leader.

---

112 Emmett Murphy, *The Genius of Sitting Bull* (New Jersey: Prentice-Hall), 1993.

Custer was so consumed with himself that he did not develop a necessary team approach to winning battles. Instead, Murphy notes that leaders like General Custer begin to believe in their own unproven ability to make decisions (referred to as hubris). Ironically, as one flawed decision justifies another in their own eyes, they begin to feel self-righteously invincible until they make one final decision that inflicts tragic consequences on those even around them.[113]

In 1868, Custer abandoned his troops during a battle with Cheyenne Indians after a previous sneak attack on a Cheyenne village. As a result, Major Joel Elliot and 16 soldiers were killed. As Murphy notes, Custer's abandonment of Elliot would reap scorn from officers and soldiers in his command.[114]

Conversely, his opponent Sitting Bull did not make decisions based solely on his prestigious Chief status. He chose instead to build a coalition of other independent tribes and their chiefs to eventually defeat General Custer at Little Bighorn.[115]

Sitting Bull would often take the lead at council meetings but consciously reached out to the other leaders to seek their opinions. According to Murphy, "Sitting Bull understood that each leader and tribe needed to reach the same conclusion he had himself reached, but not on his authority alone."[116]

In the end, Sitting Bull achieved victory by making decisions based on his mission of including everyone involved to defeat the invading army. Custer, on the other hand, goes down in American folklore defeated like no other General in our military history.

Final Thoughts on using the APE Theory

As you have seen, there are numerous principles embodied in this tenth and last principle, using the APE theory. The acronym is an easy-to-remember way to understand the importance of starting with yourself and branching out to partner with others, and finally to all

---

113 Ibid.
114 Ibid.
115 Ibid.
116 Ibid.

people (everyone) so that they can contribute.

The concept is essentially an *inside-outside* approach. By being a person of character, who holds himself or herself accountable, you are role modeling good behavior for others. That behavior builds trust with others, especially teammates who will see that you are not only about achieving success for yourself. You are demonstrating leadership maturity when you do so. Finally, you are inclusive and recognize that diversity is a strength. Every single person in the organization should be allowed to participate so they can contribute, including creative ideas to solve problems.

Conclusion

"Graduation is a time of completion, of finishing, of an ending, however, it is also a time of celebration of achievement and a beginning for the new graduate."

Catherine Pulsifer, author

OBTAINING A COLLEGE degree is a life-changing milestone. Sometimes there is an immediate outcome (an officer commission for service academy graduates), while for others it may take a little while. Regardless, there should always be the personal gratification that comes from graduating from college.

In my college days, I would often play in my mind running a 400-meter hurdle race. There are ten evenly-spaced hurdles that must be cleared once around the track. The hurdles represented obstacles I needed to overcome to "finish the race" and graduate from college. Sometimes a hurdle represented finding the resources to continue with my education. Another hurdle was to navigate registration and sign-up for the necessary courses to complete degree requirements. Still another hurdle (or two) represented some tough classes that I barely cleared, but nevertheless, made it over and continued the race. Whatever your hurdles were along the way, you have reached the finish line and cleared the tape. Nothing can take that hard-earned accomplishment away from you.

For many, you were also first generation, meaning nobody else in your family completed or even attended college. That was my case, and I am especially proud to lead the way for others in my family to see a college degree as attainable.

When you hear those magic words, "By authority of …..I confer the degree to the candidates," a tremendous milestone is reached. At this time, or perhaps another time during the commencement ceremony, it is tradition that graduates throw their caps high in the air to celebrate. Enjoy your moment with great pride and satisfaction.

My purpose in writing this book is not to put a damper on the celebration. In fact, I celebrate with all of you. Rather, my goal is that when the graduation cap falls, you start a new chapter in life. One with wonderful challenges and rewards that comes with a college degree.

The ten principles I offer you have worked for me, across a variety of circumstances. My hope is that one, several, or all ten, will help you in some way as you continue upward in your career path.

Congratulations graduate.

The world is eager for you to make a difference.

Acknowledgements

To my beautiful and loving wife Brenda, who is my inspiration in all endeavors. To Dr. Connie Book, President at Elon University, for writing the books' foreword, taking the time out of her busy schedule shows that she is the kind of leader that makes me proud to call her a colleague and friend. Thanks to Tom Stock for the photo. A special thanks to all the students in my leadership classes, and especially the ones who wrote their testimonies for this book.

www.ingramcontent.com/pod-product-compliance
Lightning Source LLC
Chambersburg PA
CBHW070241230526
45470CB00002B/471